ALPHABET

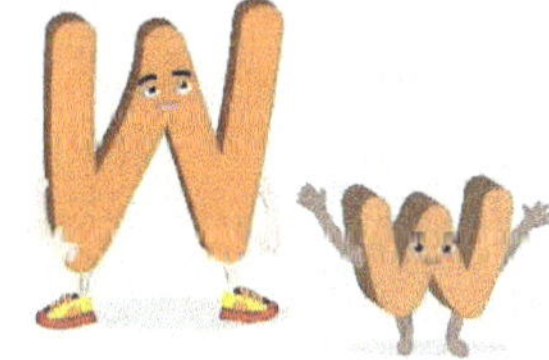
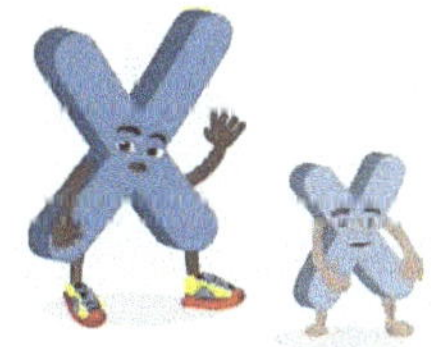

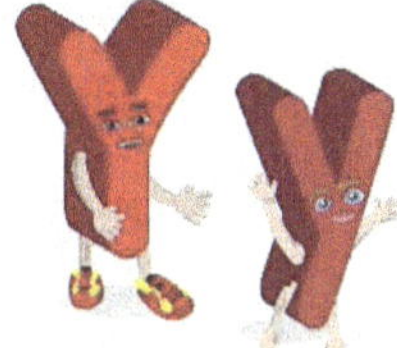

10 9 8 7 6 5 4 3 2 1

First published 2022 with a non-exclusive licence from the authors to CHEETAH® Purrrrrrr Publishing, an imprint of CHEETAH® Toys & More, LLC (CHEETAH®).

ISBN-13: 979-8-88589-395-4
ISBN-10:   8-88589-395-4

Permission requests should be submitted to the publisher in writing via email at info@mycheetahacademy.com or paulettetrowers@yahoo.com.

CHEETAH® Toys & More, LLC
207 Main Street, 3rd Floor
Hartford, CT 06106

Port Antonio P.O.
Portland, Jamaica

info@mycheetahacademy.com
paulettetrowers@yahoo.com
WhatsApp: 876-909-6311

Authors: Rosemarie Pottinger, Kristina Jaz, Fiona Porter-Lawson
Editors: Fiona Porter-Lawson, Patricia Bryan
Cover and interior design: CHEETAH® Purrrrrrr Publishing ("CHEETAH®"), an imprint of CHEETAH® Toys & More, LLC.
Publisher: CHEETAH® (Connect to Higher Education, Electronic Tools, Application & Help)
www.mycheetahacademy.com

Table of contents

About this book

CHEETAH® Early Childhood Phonics for 5-year-olds is the third in a series of phonics books designed for young learners.

This text is aligned with the Jamaica Early Childhood Curriculum Guide for 5-year-olds that was created by the Early Childhood Commission and as such, incorporates the themes and sub-themes used throughout the curriculum.

We believe that integrating aspects of the curriculum in a beginning phonics textbook will make the teacher's task easier and the pupils' learning experience more fulfilling.

The book is divided into two main parts:

1. alphabet: this includes consonants and vowels (long and short as treated in the curriculum)
2. clusters: the curriculum treats a few digraphs and blends: ch, cl, pl, sh, st and th.

Features

Each letter and cluster is presented in its own section. Each section begins with examples from the curriculum and a sample image.

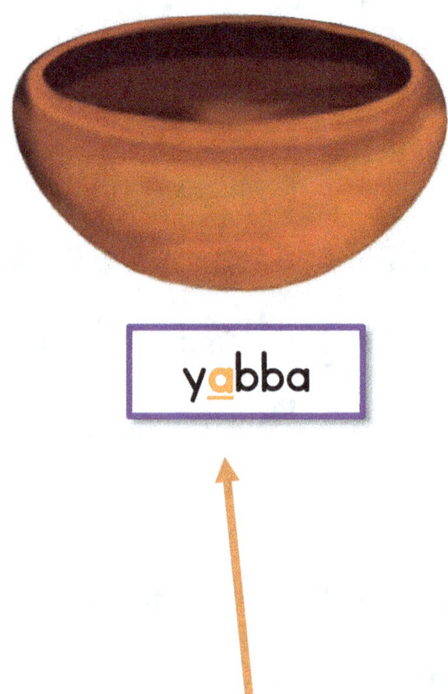

yabba

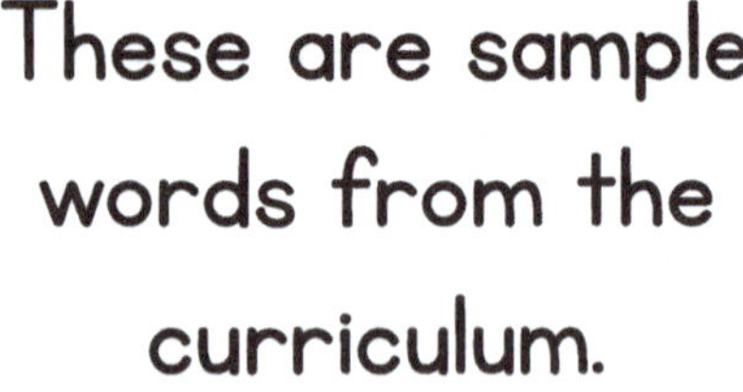

These are sample words from the curriculum.

This is a sample image.

Features

Sounds appear in one, two or three positions in a word: initial, medial and final position.

We included samples in the section named *Say my name.*

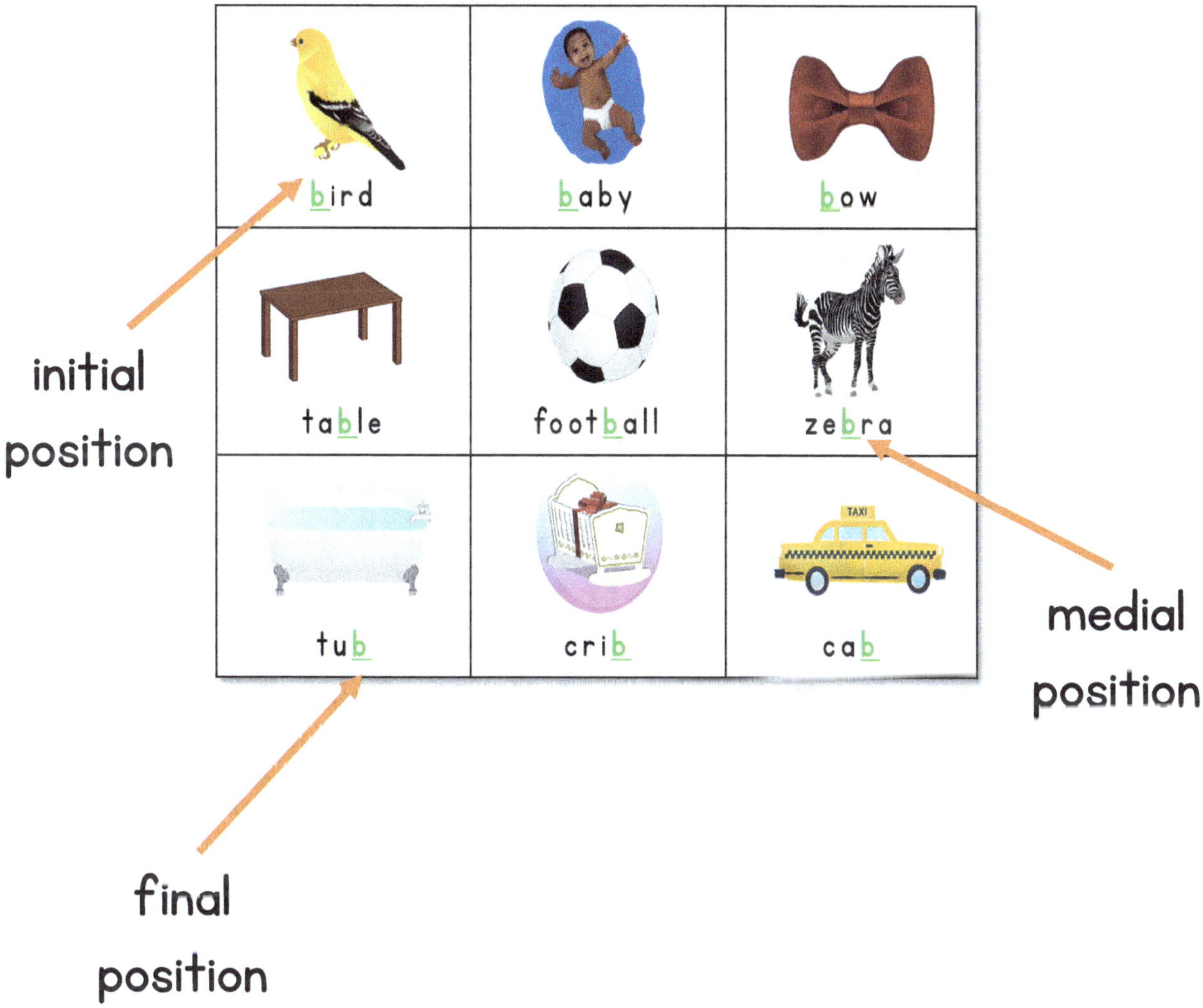

b<u>i</u>rd	<u>b</u>aby	<u>b</u>ow
ta<u>b</u>le	foot<u>b</u>all	ze<u>b</u>ra
tu<u>b</u>	cri<u>b</u>	ca<u>b</u>

initial position

medial position

final position

Features

Each section contains seven activities including a full-length picture story.

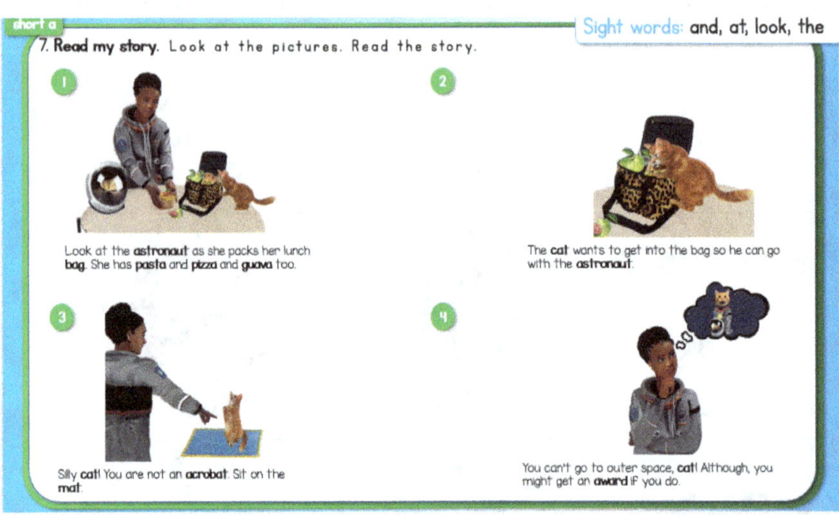

Can you hear the sound?

An essential skill in learning new concepts is checking how much one has learnt. At the end of each chapter, pupils will reflect on their progress.

They will select (orally) one of the following statements:

1. 'Yes, I can!'

This statement tells us that the pupil is very comfortable with the concept and can move on to the next.

Yes, I can!

2. 'Not sure.'

If the pupil expresses this statement, we know the pupil needs more exposure to this concept.

Not sure.

3. 'No, I can't.'

This statement tells us we need to revisit this concept.

No, I can't!

Activity formats

Say my name: Pupils look at and name each object.

Find my name: First, pupils look at the words in the word bank at the top of the page. They then look at each picture and locate its name in the bank. Finally, they write the name of the picture in the space provided.

Check me: Pupils identify the image on the left. They look for the name of the image and check the box beside it. They will then write the name of the image in the space provided.

Read me: Pupils read the sentence using the images as guides.

Circle my name: Pupils look at the picture on the left and circle its name on the right.

Trace my name: This activity is two-fold. In the first instance, pupils look at the pictures on the left and then the word on the right. They then circle the picture that the word names. In the space provided, pupils trace the name at the top and then write the same name at the bottom.

Activity formats

Find my letters: Pupils look at the picture, circle the letters that are in its name and then write/trace its name in the space provided.

Add my letter: Pupils look at both pictures and then at the letters that are between the pictures. They use their knowledge of how the name of each picture is spelt to complete the word. They then circle the picture that the word names.

Match my parts: Pupils look at the image then circle the word parts that form the name of the image.

Circle then write my name: Pupils look at the picture and circle its name. They then write the name of the picture.

Write my name: Pupils use the picture as a clue to complete the sentence.

Activity formats

Unscramble me: Pupils unscramble the letters to form the name of the picture. Then they write the correct name in the space provided.

Match me: Pupils match the image with its name, then write in the missing letters in the name.

Read my story: Pupils read the story. They use the image to help figure out what is happening in the story.

Snapshot of letters/sounds as outlined in the curriculum

Term	Theme	Sub-theme	Letters
1	Our country Jamaica – Our people	Our people from Africa	m, short a
		Our people from India	short i
		Our people from Europe	s
		Our people from the Middle East	p
		Our people from China	ch, n
2	Transportation	Types of transportation	h, l
		Getting ready for a flight	hard c
		At the airport	d
2	Transportation	In the harbour	sh
	Sports	Let's exercise	st, short e
		We love to play	u, pl, cl
		Famous Jamaicans in sports	g, r

3	Jamaica land we love	The beauty of our land	th, sh
		Interesting Jamaicans	long a
		Our visitors	long e
3	The weather	What is the weather like?	w, long o
		Dressing for the weather	u
		Whether the weather	z

Learning and teaching begin with CHEETAH®.

"Now, therefore, who teach another, do you not teach yourself?" Romans 2:21 (NJKV).

Sub-theme: Our people from Africa

Term I

short /a/: initial, medial and ending positions

Aa

Africa

katt**a**

y**a**bba

y**a**bba

short /a/ sound

1. **Say my name.** Point to each word. Say its name.

astronaut	**a**nt	**a**crobat
m**a**t	b**a**g	c**a**t
apple	**a**lligator	past**a**

2. **Find my name.** Find its name in the box and write it on the lines.

Word bank

cat	ant	alligator

ant

short /a/ sound

3. Check me. Look at the picture. Check the name. Write the name.

☐ <u>a</u>stronaut ☑ <u>a</u>crobat ☐ <u>a</u>nt

☐ yabb<u>a</u> ☐ past<u>a</u> ☐ <u>a</u>pple

☐ b<u>a</u>g ☐ c<u>a</u>t ☐ m<u>a</u>t

4. Read me. Read the sentence.

The <u>a</u>stronaut will give the past<u>a</u> to the c<u>a</u>t.

short /a/ sound

5. Circle my name. Circle the name of the picture.

c a t   b a g   (m a t)

a s t r o n a u t   a c r o b a t   a c k e e

p a s t a   a n t   y a b b a

apple   c a t   a c r o b a t

6. Find my letters. Circle the letters then write the name.

	s (b) t		**bag**
	(g) (a)		
	a w t		
	c o		
	s t a		
	p a n		
	t m a		
	g b		

| short /a/ sound | Story words: acrobat, astronaut, bag, cat, mat, pasta |

7. Read my story. Look at the pictures. Read the story.

1

Look at the astronaut. She packs her lunch bag. She has pasta, pizza and guava.

2

The cat wants to get into the bag. He wants to go with the astronaut.

3

"Silly cat! You are not an acrobat. Sit on the mat."

4

"You can't go to outer space, cat! But you may get an award if you do."

Say these words.
Africa
katta
yabba
Can you hear the /a/ sound?
Yes, I can!
Not sure.
No, I can't.

Term 3 — long /ā/ sound: ai. Extended learning: ay, a_e (vcv)

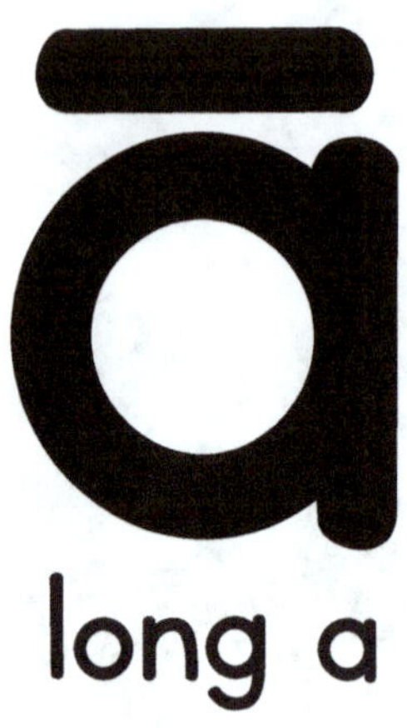

ā

long a

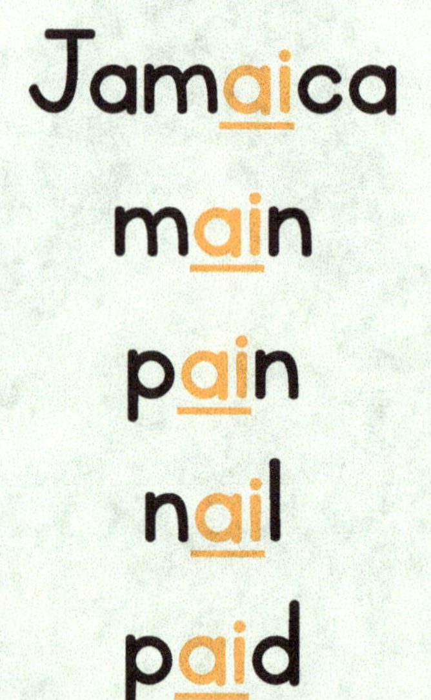

long /ā/ sound

1. **Say my name.** Point to each picture. Say its name.

rain	snail	train
pray	play	ray
gate	plane	wave

2. **Find my name.** Find its name in the box and write it on the lines.

Word bank

plane   train   play

train

3. **Match my parts**. Circle the parts to make the name.

tr
ain
r

r
pl
ay

c
w
a v e

tr
r
ain

4. **Find my letters**. Circle the letters then write the name.

r   b   s

y   a

ray

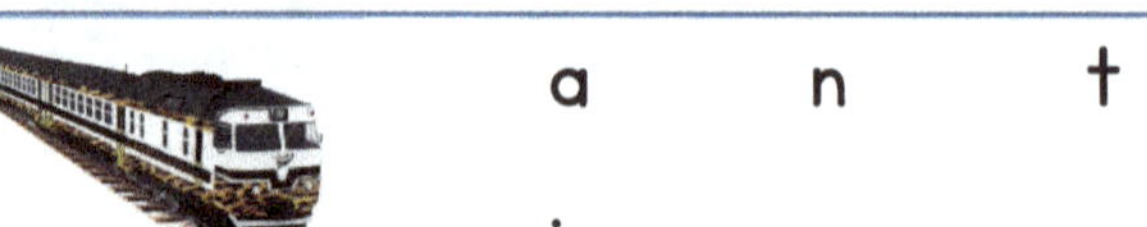

a   n   s

r   i

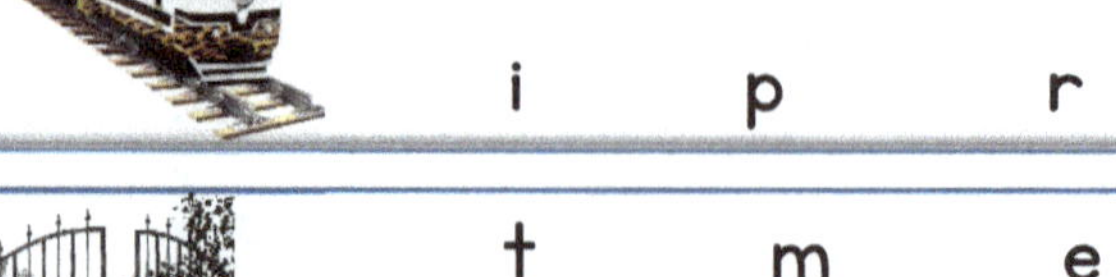

a   n   t

i   p   r

t   m   e

g   a

5. Circle then write my name. Look at the picture. Circle its name. Write its name.

play
(pray)

pray

rain
snail

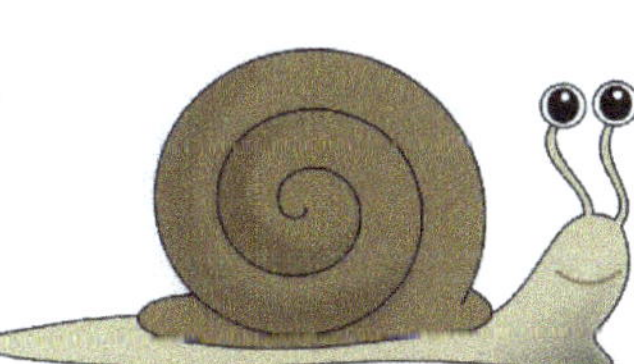

gate
plane

6. Read me. Read the sentence.

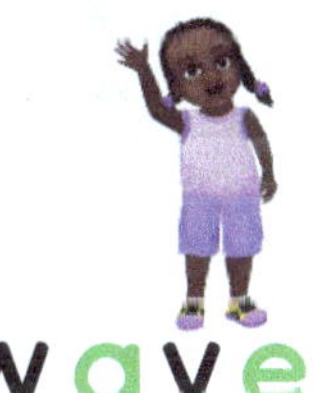

Stand at the gate and wave

at the train.

long /ā/ sound

Story words: gate, plane, play, pray, rain, rays, snail, train, wave

7. **Read my story**. Look at the pictures. Read the story.

1

Jane likes to play outside with her train and plane. The sun's rays warm her up.

2

She prays it doesn't rain.

3

Jane watches a snail crawl on the gate.

4

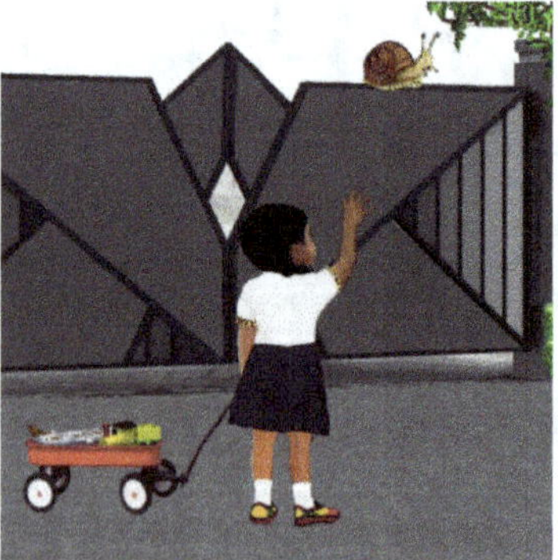

Jane waves at the snail and plays with her toys.

Say these words.
nail
paid
pain
Can you hear the long a sound?
Yes, I can!
Not sure.
No, I can't.

Term 1

/b/ sound: initial, medial and final positions

/b/ sound

1. Say my name. Point to each word. Say its name.

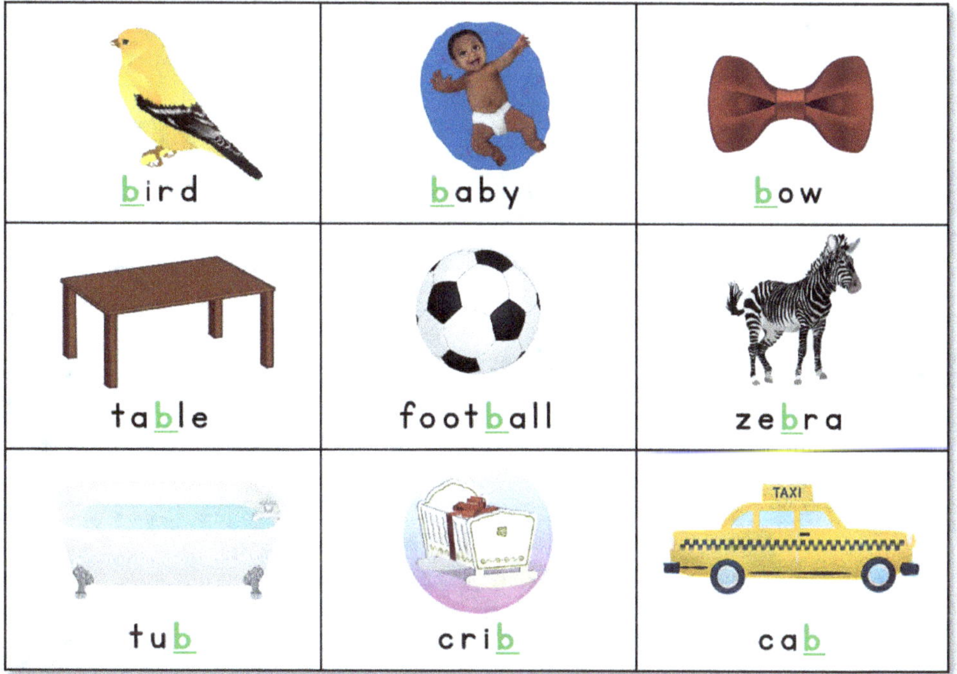

bird	**b**aby	**b**ow
ta**b**le	foot**b**all	ze**b**ra
tu**b**	cri**b**	ca**b**

2. Circle my name. Circle the name of the picture.

	ca**b** (tu**b**) cri**b** ta**b**le
	ta**b**le cri**b** ze**b**ra foot**b**all
	ze**b**ra **b**aby **b**ird **b**ow
	tu**b** **b**ow **b**aby **b**ird

/b/ sound

3. **Add my letter**. Write the word. Circle the picture.

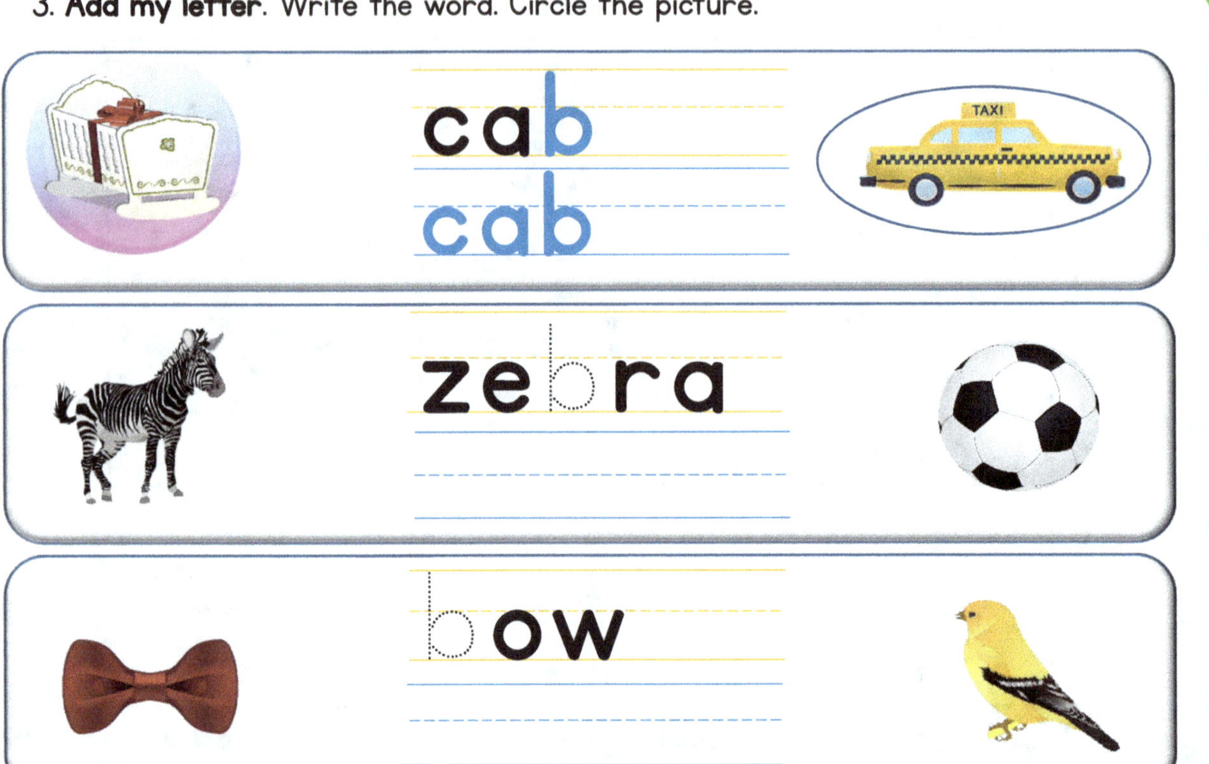

4. **Match me**. Fill in the missing letter. Match the picture and its name.

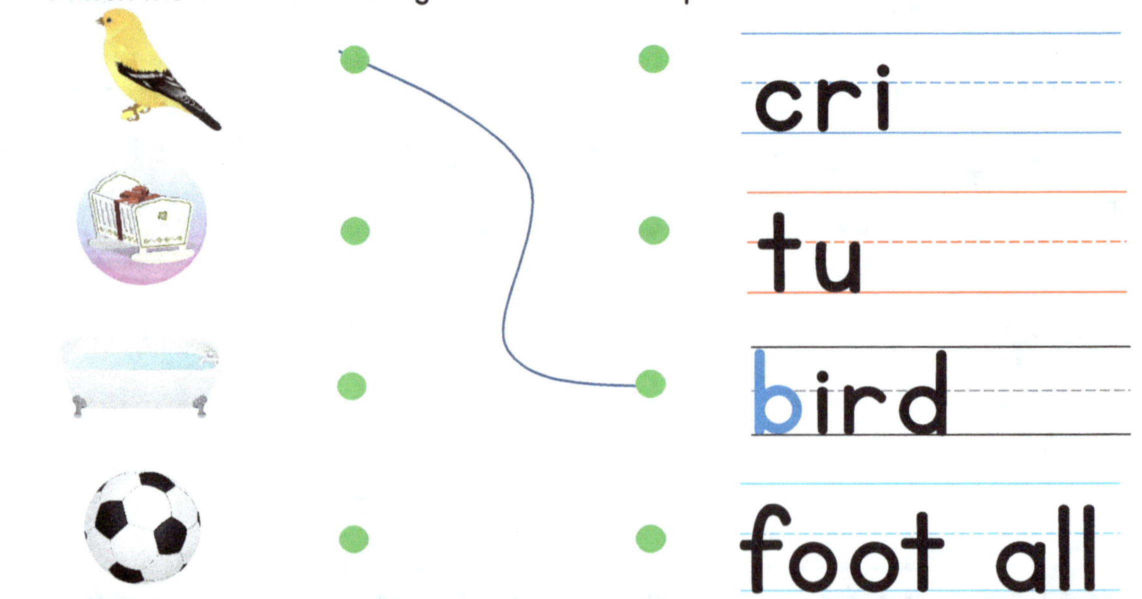

/b/ sound

5. Unscramble me. Look at the picture. Unscramble the word to form its name.

o b w 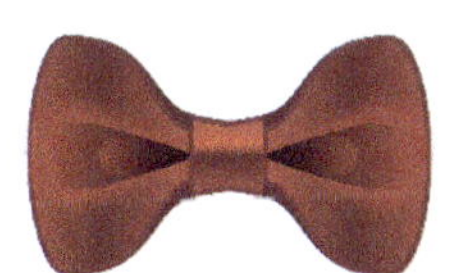 bow

a b c  ________

b t l e a  ________

6. Read me. Read the sentence.

Put the **b**aby in the cri**b**

by the ta**b**le.

/b/ sound

Story words: baby, bird, bow, cab, crib, football. tub. zebra

7. Read my story. Look at the pictures. Read the story.

Baby Bird loves to play football with his friend zebra.

He scores a goal. Take a bow, Baby Bird.

Later, he plays with his yellow toy cab as he bathes in the tub.

Look at Baby Bird now fast asleep in his crib.

Say these words.
cab
fabric
bead
Can you hear the /b/ sound?
Yes, I can!
Not sure.
No, I can't.

Theme: Transportation

Sub-theme: Getting ready for a flight

Term 2

hard 'c' sound /k/: initial, medial and final positions

Cc
car
cap
car

hard 'c' sound /k/

1. Say my name. Point to each picture. Say its name.

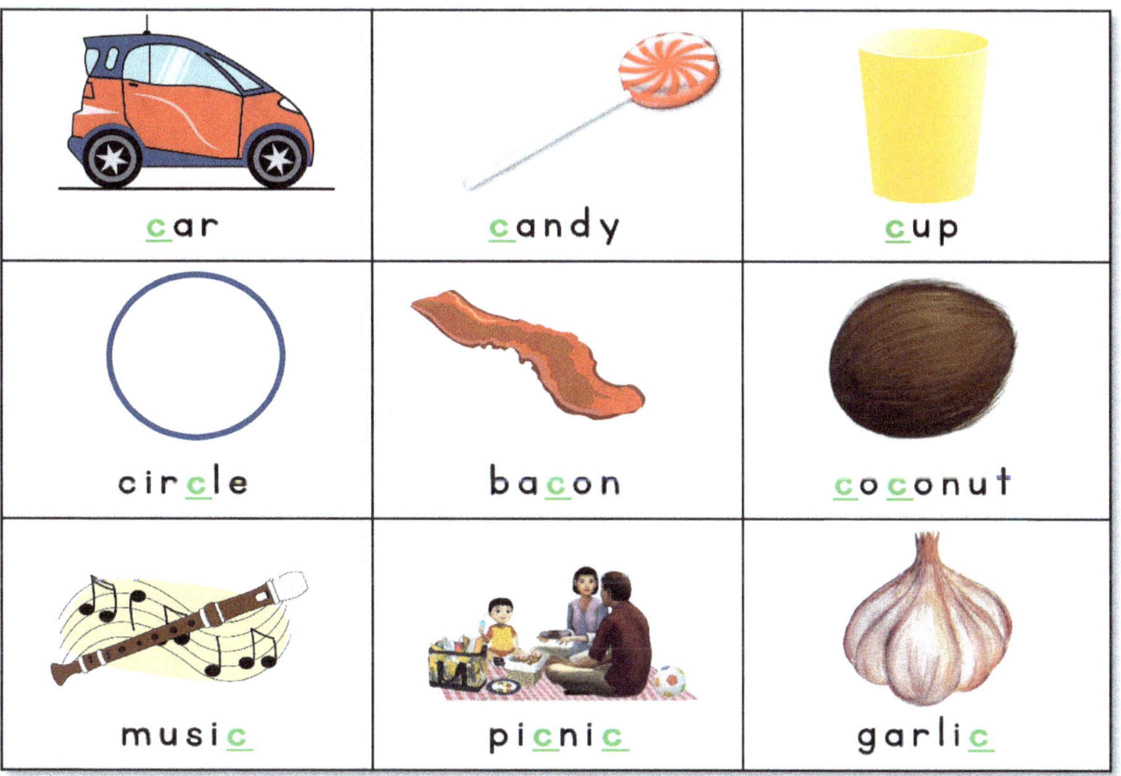

2. Match me. Fill in the missing letter. Match the picture and its name.

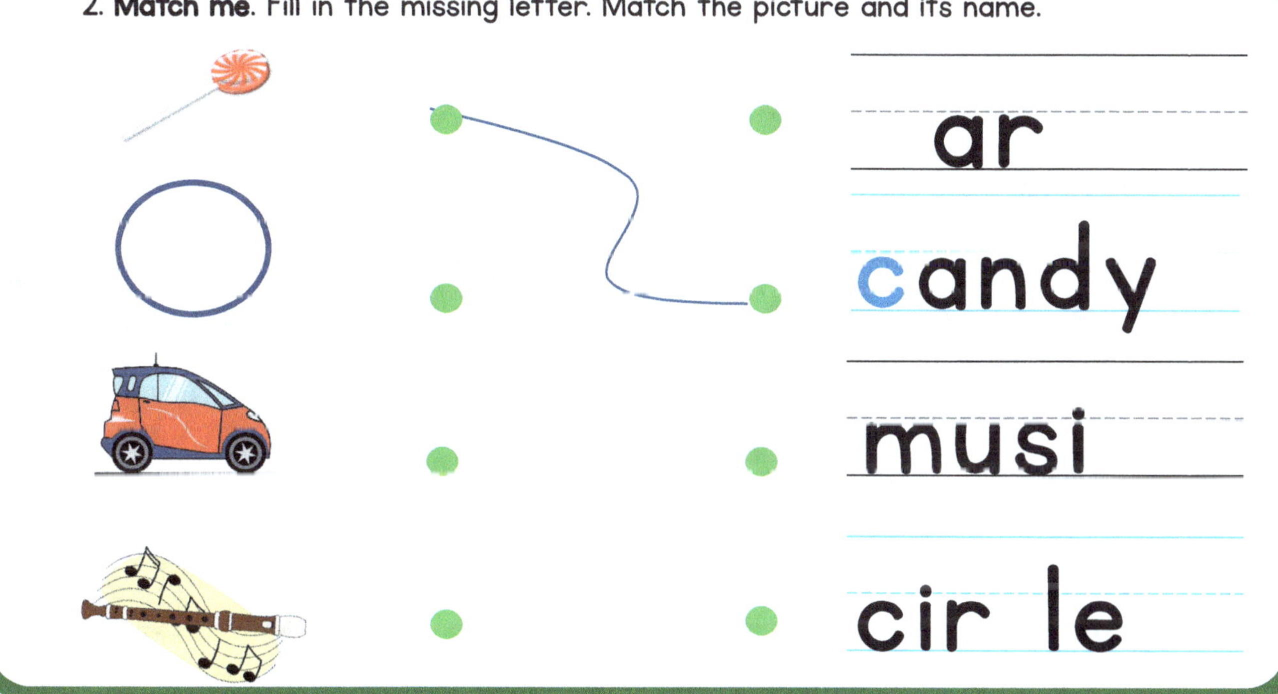

hard 'c' sound /k/

3. **Check me**. Look at the picture. Check the name. Write the name.

☐ cir**c**le   ☑ ba**c**on   ☐ **c**o**c**onut

bacon

☐ garli**c**   ☐ pi**c**ni**c**   ☐ musi**c**

☐ **c**ar   ☐ **c**up   ☐ **c**andy

4. **Read me**. Read the sentence.

There are **c**o**c**onuts and **c**andy at the pi**c**ni**c**.

hard 'c' sound /k/

5. Add my letter. Write the word. Circle the picture.

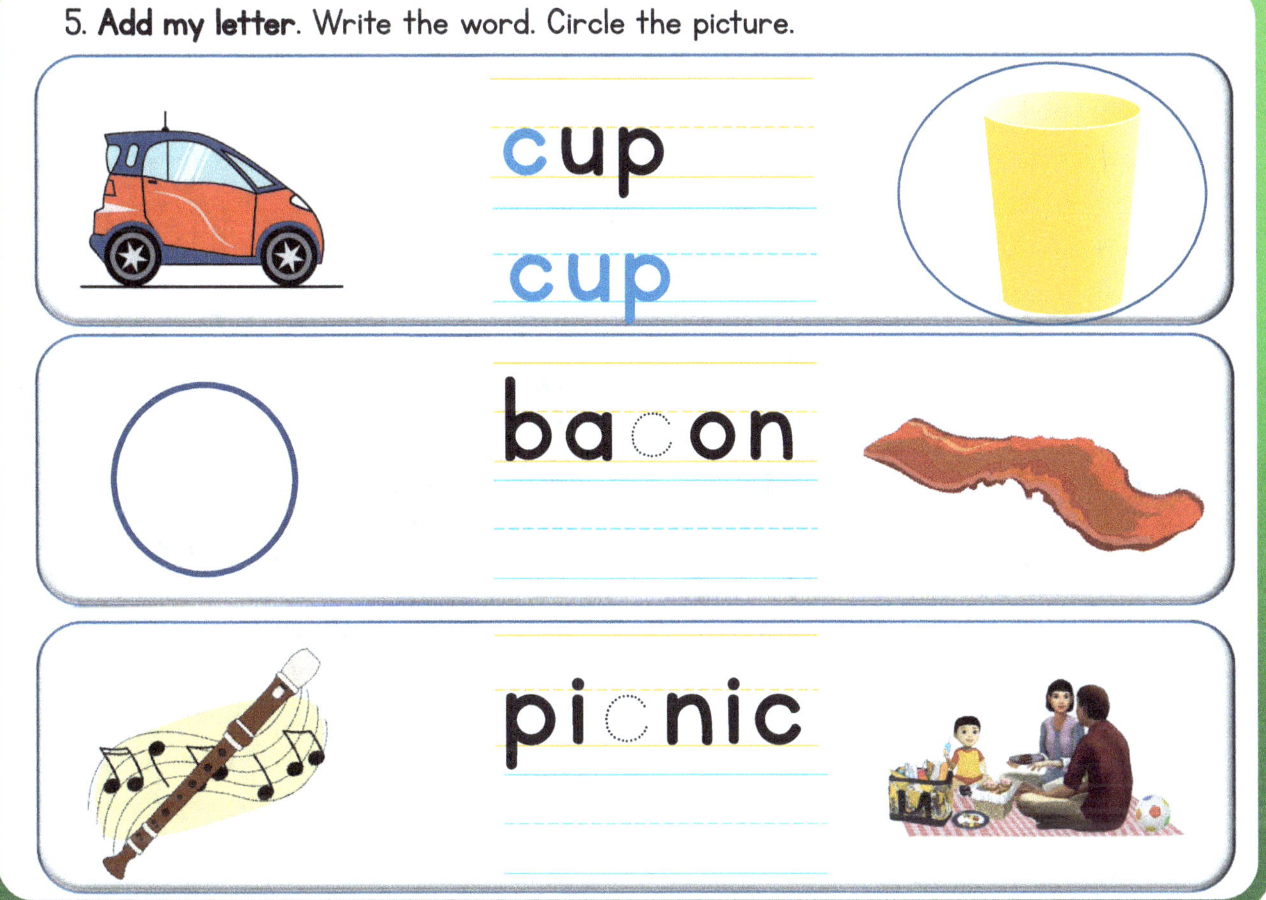

cup

cup

bac on

picnic

6. Write my name. Write the name in the sentence.

I like candy .

__________ are brown.

hard 'c' sound /k/

Story words: bacon, candy, car, circle, coconut, cup, garlic, music, picnic

7. **Read my story.** Look at the pictures. Read the story.

1

Let's drive our car to the park!

2

Let us ride bumper cars in circles as the music plays.

3

Let us have a picnic with coconut cakes, garlic bread, bacon and candy.

4

And a big cup of juice to wash it down.

Say these words.
cup
car
Can you hear the hard 'c' sound /k/?
Yes, I can!
Not sure.
No, I can't.

Theme: Transportation

Sub-theme: At the airport

Term 2

/d/ sound: initial, medial and final positions

Dd

departure
load
board
medal

board

/d/ sound

1. Say my name. Point to each picture. Say its name.

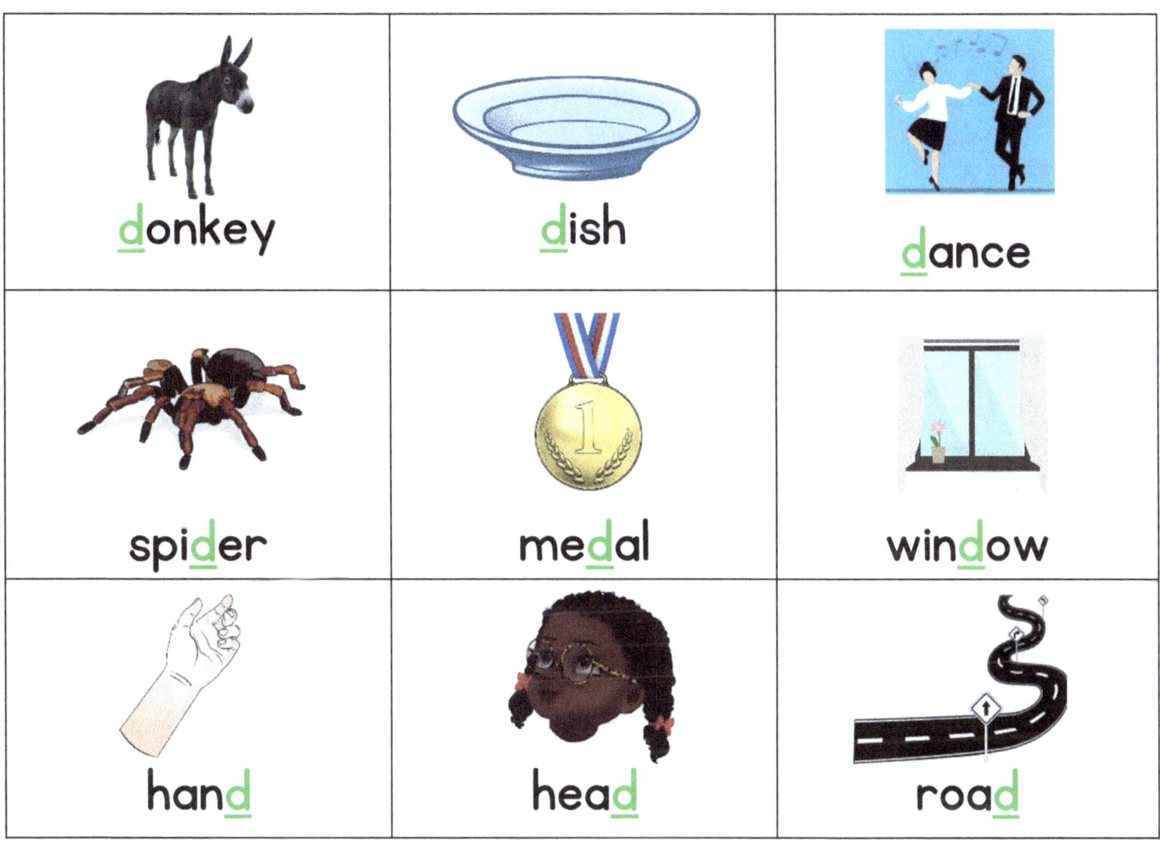

donkey	**d**ish	**d**ance
spi**d**er	me**d**al	win**d**ow
han**d**	hea**d**	roa**d**

2. Circle my name. Circle the name of the picture.

roa**d**   **d**ish   (hea**d**)   win**d**ow

spi**d**er   roa**d**   win**d**ow   han**d**

me**d**al   **d**ance   **d**onkey   roa**d**

hea**d**   **d**ish   spi**d**er   han**d**

3. **Match me**. Fill in the missing letter. Match the picture and its name.

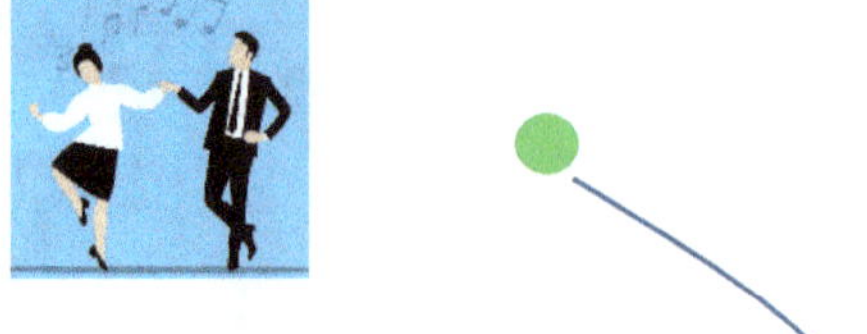

ish

onkey

dance

spi er

4. **Find my letters**. Circle the letters then write the name.

	n b d / h a o	hand
	c h a / g d e	____________
	d i a / m l e	____________
	i n d g / w s o w	____________

5. Unscramble me. Look at the picture. Unscramble the word to form its name.

o r d a  road

s h i d 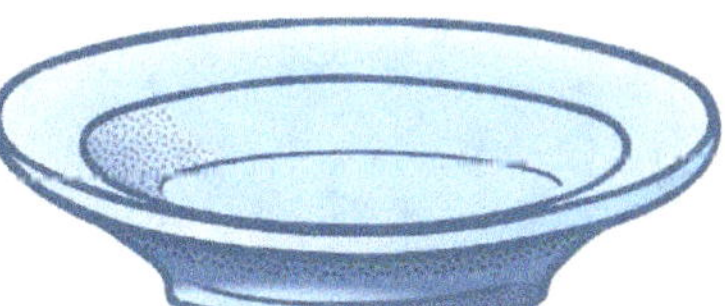

m l d e a 

6. Read me. Read the sentence.

Hold han**d**s and **d**ance

beside the win**d**ow.

/d/ sound

Story words: dance, dish, donkey, hand, head, medal, road, spider

7. **Read my story**. Look at the pictures. Read the story.

1

Look! A donkey and a spider are dancing on the bridge.

2

I wave my hands and dance on the road too.

3

Will I get a medal or a dish of sweets?

4

Will the donkey and spider get too?

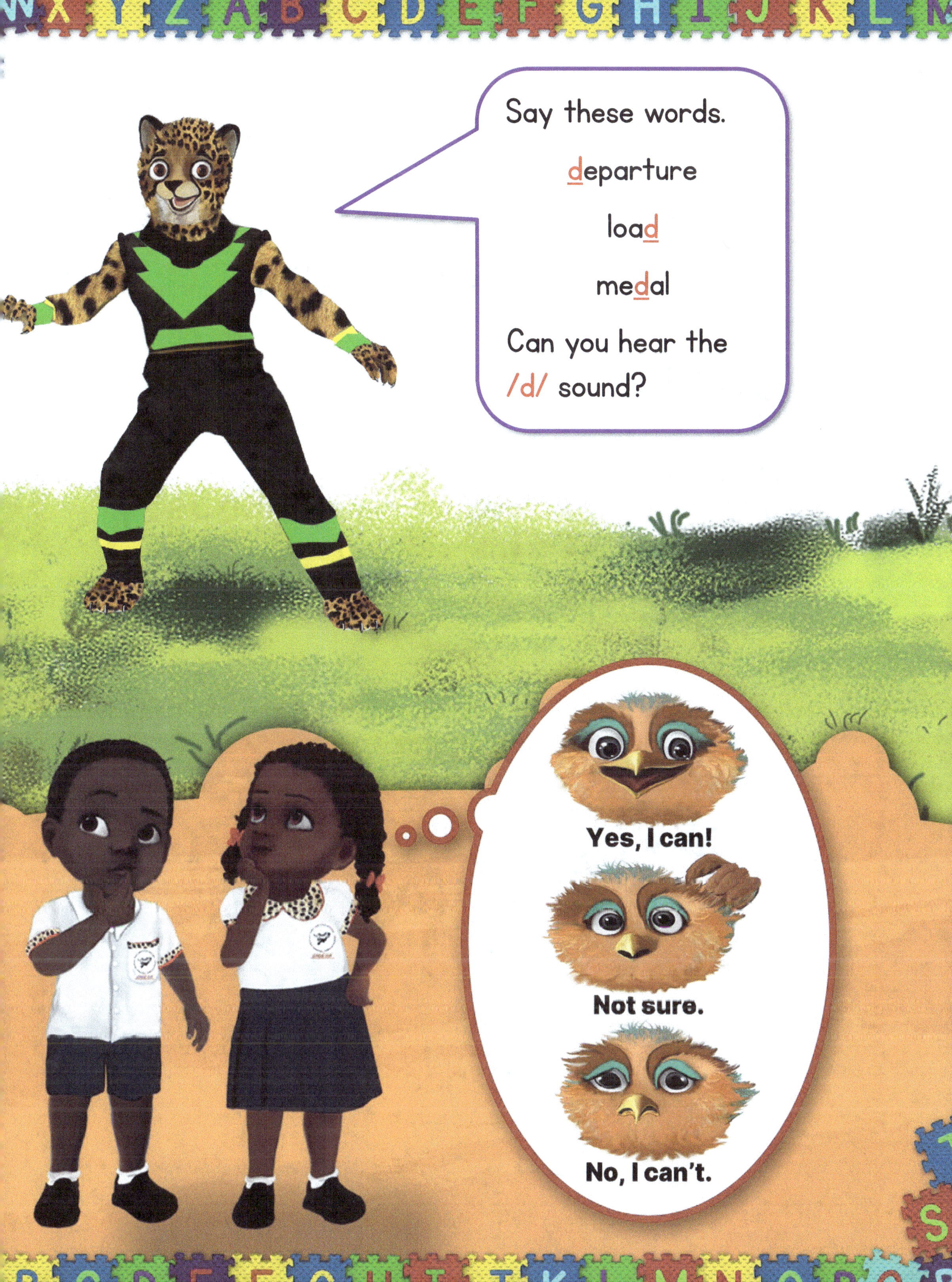
Say these words.
departure
load
medal
Can you hear the
/d/ sound?
Yes, I can!
Not sure.
No, I can't.

Term 2

short /e/ sound: initial and medial positions

Ee

short /e/ sound

1. Say my name. Point to each picture. Say its name.

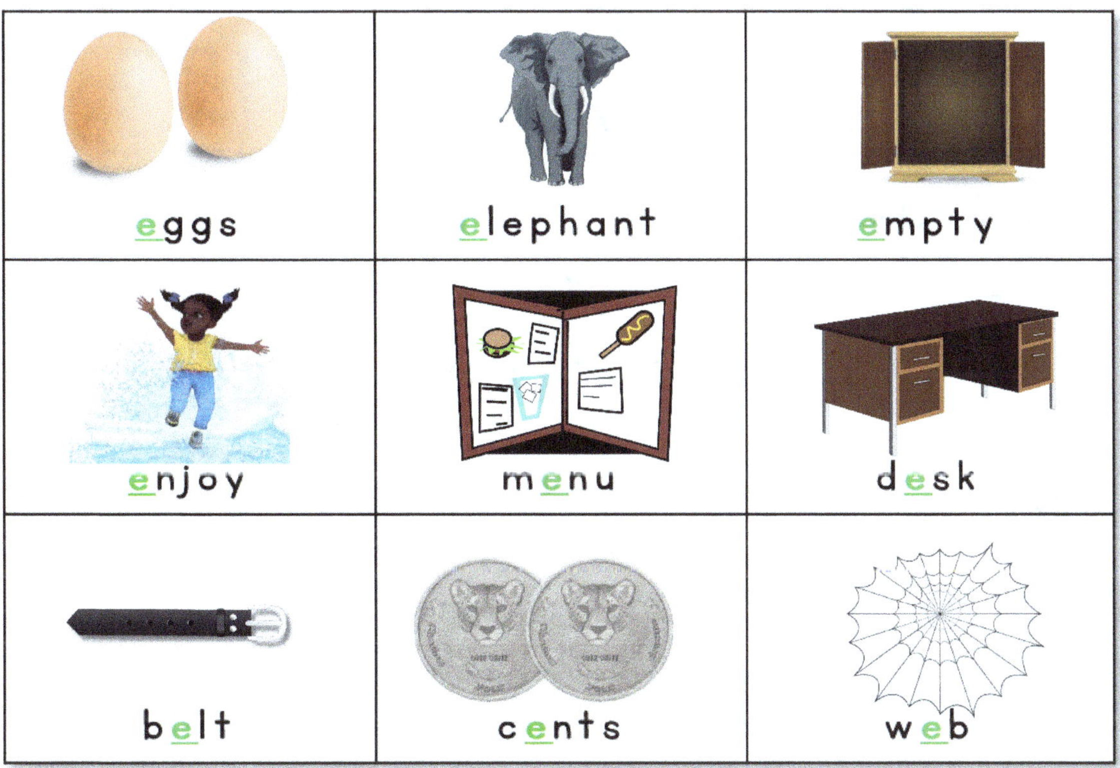

2. Match me. Fill in the missing letter. Match the picture and its name.

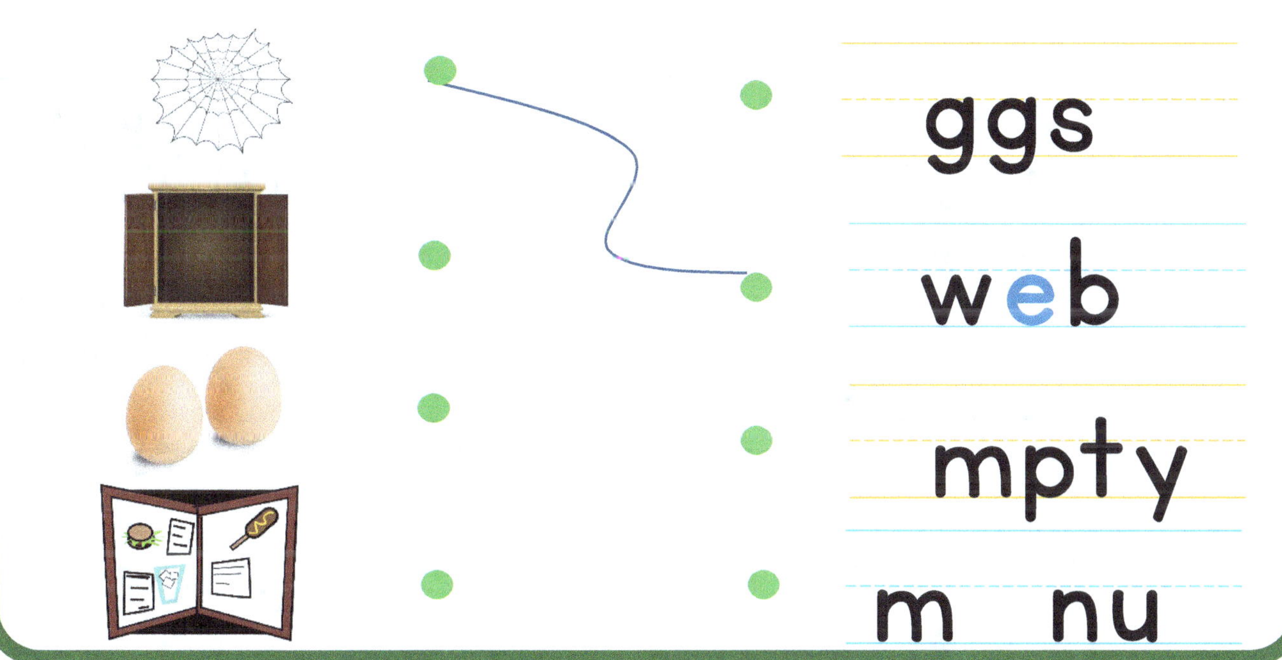

3. **Add my letter.** Write the word. Circle the picture.

 **w e b** 

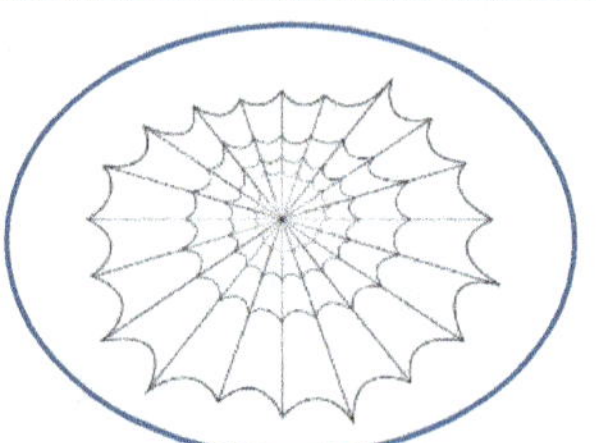 **e lephant**

 **c e nts** 

4. **Write my name.** Write the name in the sentence.

Sit at the **desk**. 

See the __________. 

 __________ your day!   

short /e/ sound

5. Check me. Look at the picture. Check the name. Write the name.

☐ m **e** n u   ☑ b **e** l t   ☐ w **e** b

belt

☐ **e** m p t y   ☐ **e** g g s   ☐ **e** n j o y

☐ c **e** n t s   ☐ d **e** s k   ☐ **e** l e p h a n t

6. Read me. Read the sentence.

W **e** bs are in the **e** mpty

d **e** sk.

Story words: belt, cents, desk, eggs, elephant, lemon, menu, web

7. Read my story. Look at the pictures. Read the story.

1

Mrs Spider is on her web. The web is under the desk.

2

She is hungry. "Do I want eggs and lemon pie?" she says.

3

She goes to the restaurant and an elephant gives her a menu.

"Do I pay with my bag of cents?" she says.

4

"Will I break my belt after I eat?"

Say these words.
exercise
friends
rest
Can you hear the
short /e/ sound?
Yes, I can!
Not sure.
No, I can't.

Term 3 — long /ē/ sound: ee   Extended learning: ea, ey

ē

long e

long /ē/ sound

1. Say my name. Point to each picture. Say its name.

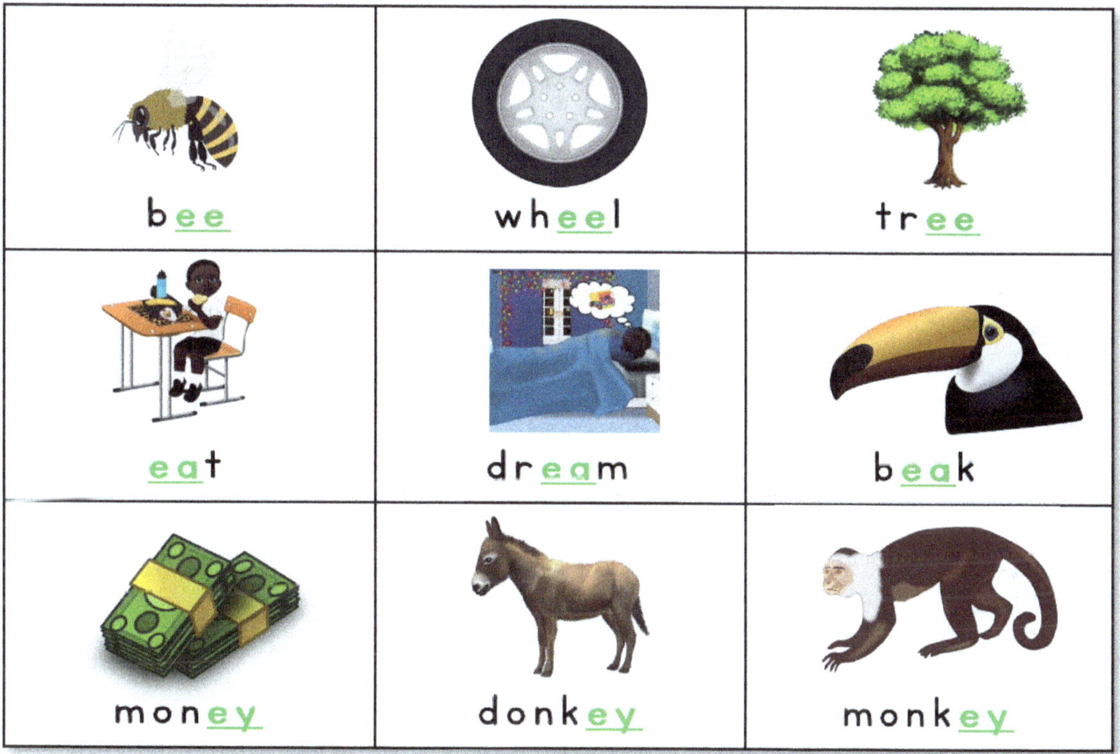

2. Match my parts. Circle the parts to make the name.

long /ē/ sound

3. **Trace my name.** Circle the picture. Trace its name.

 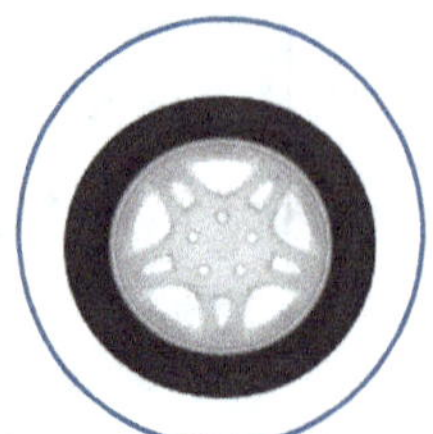  
wheel

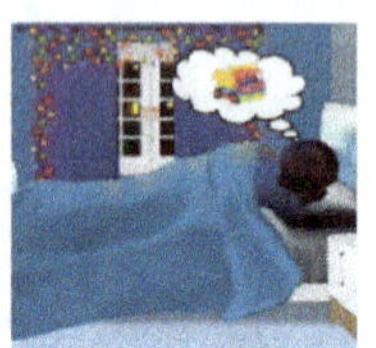   
eat

money

4. **Find my name.** Say the word. Write its name.

Word bank

| tree | dream | bee |

bee

5. Circle then write my name. Look at the picture. Circle its name. Write its name.

wh<u>ee</u>l

tr<u>ee</u>

wheel

monk<u>ey</u>

donk<u>ey</u>

b<u>ea</u>k

dr<u>ea</u>m

6. Read me. Read the sentence.

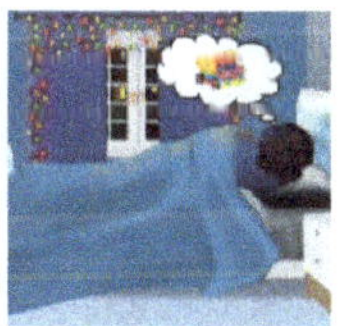

The monk<u>ey</u> had a dr<u>ea</u>m

about a tr<u>ee</u>. 

long /ē/ sound

Story words: beak, bee, donkey, dream, eat, money, monkey, street, tree, wheel

7. **Read my story**. Look at the pictures. Read the story.

1

Donkey is happy. He found money on the street. He buys honey for his friends, Monkey and Bee.

2

They go for a ride in a cart. They do not see the bird with the big beak.

3

They hit a tree and the wheels fall off!

4

Donkey jumps up. "I am glad it was just a dream."

Say these words.
seeing
green
tree
Can you hear the long
/ē/ sound?
Yes, I can!
Not sure.
No, I can't.

Sub-theme: Our people from Africa

Term 1 — /f/ sound: initial, medial and final positions

Ff

Africa
fabric
leaf

Africa

/f/ sound

1. Say my name. Point to each picture. Say its name.

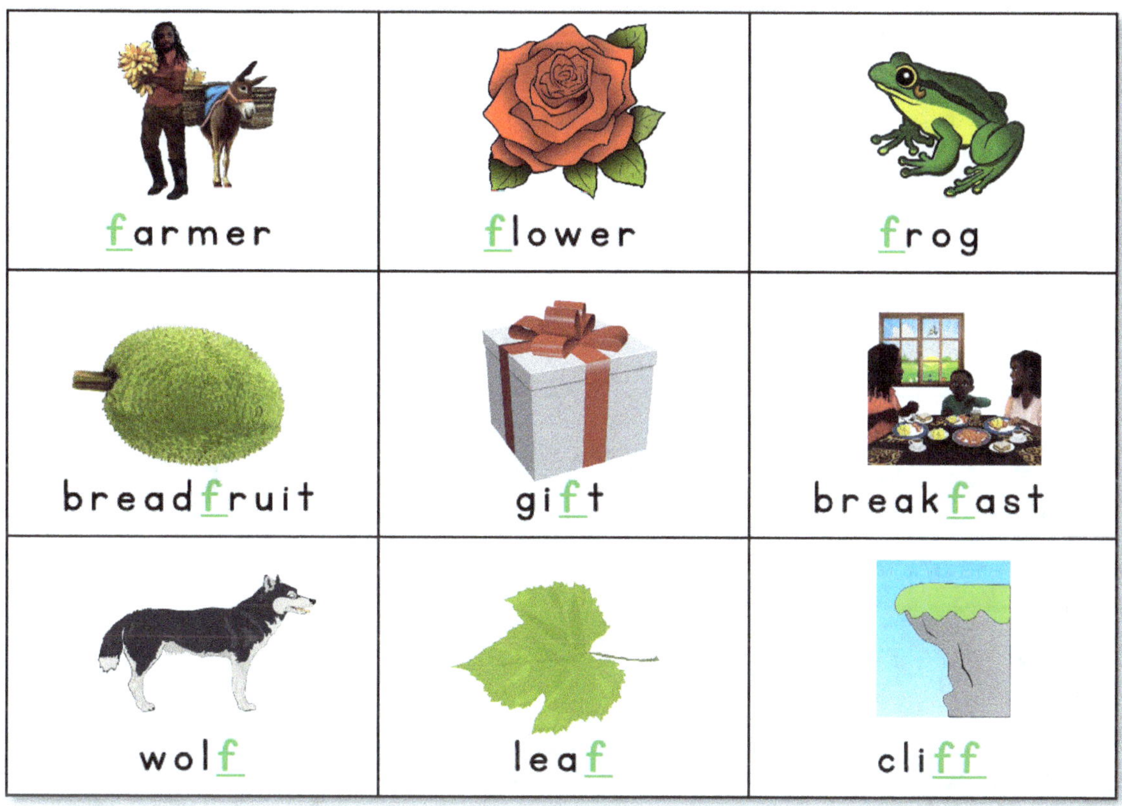

f<u>a</u>rmer	f<u>l</u>ower	f<u>r</u>og
bread<u>f</u>ruit	gi<u>f</u>t	break<u>f</u>ast
wol<u>f</u>	lea<u>f</u>	cli<u>ff</u>

2. Add my letter. Write the word. Circle the picture.

frog

gift

leaf

/f/ sound

3. Circle my name. Circle the name of the picture.

 _f_armer   (cli_ff_)   lea_f_   gi_f_t

 bread_f_ruit   _f_rog   _f_lower   _f_armer

 wol_f_   break_f_ast   bread_f_ruit   lea_f_

 _f_lower   cli_ff_   _f_rog   _f_armer

4. Write my name. Write the name in the sentence.

The **frog** is green. 

Hear the ________ howl. 

Eat the ____________. 

5. Unscramble me. Look at the picture. Unscramble the word to form its name.

f t g i      gift

a l e f   

l o r e f w   

6. Read me. Read the sentence.

Do **f**rogs eat bread**f**ruit

for break**f**ast?

/f/ sound

Story words: breadfruit, breakfast, cliff, farmer, flower, frog, gift, leaf, wolf

7. Read my story. Look at the pictures. Read the story.

The little frog climbs up a cliff.

He sees a big wolf wearing a bib.

The wolf sees the frog and offers him a flower with a green leaf.

"Here is a gift. Have breakfast with me."

A farmer under a breadfruit tree shouts, "Run, frog! Run for your life! Run so you can see another day."

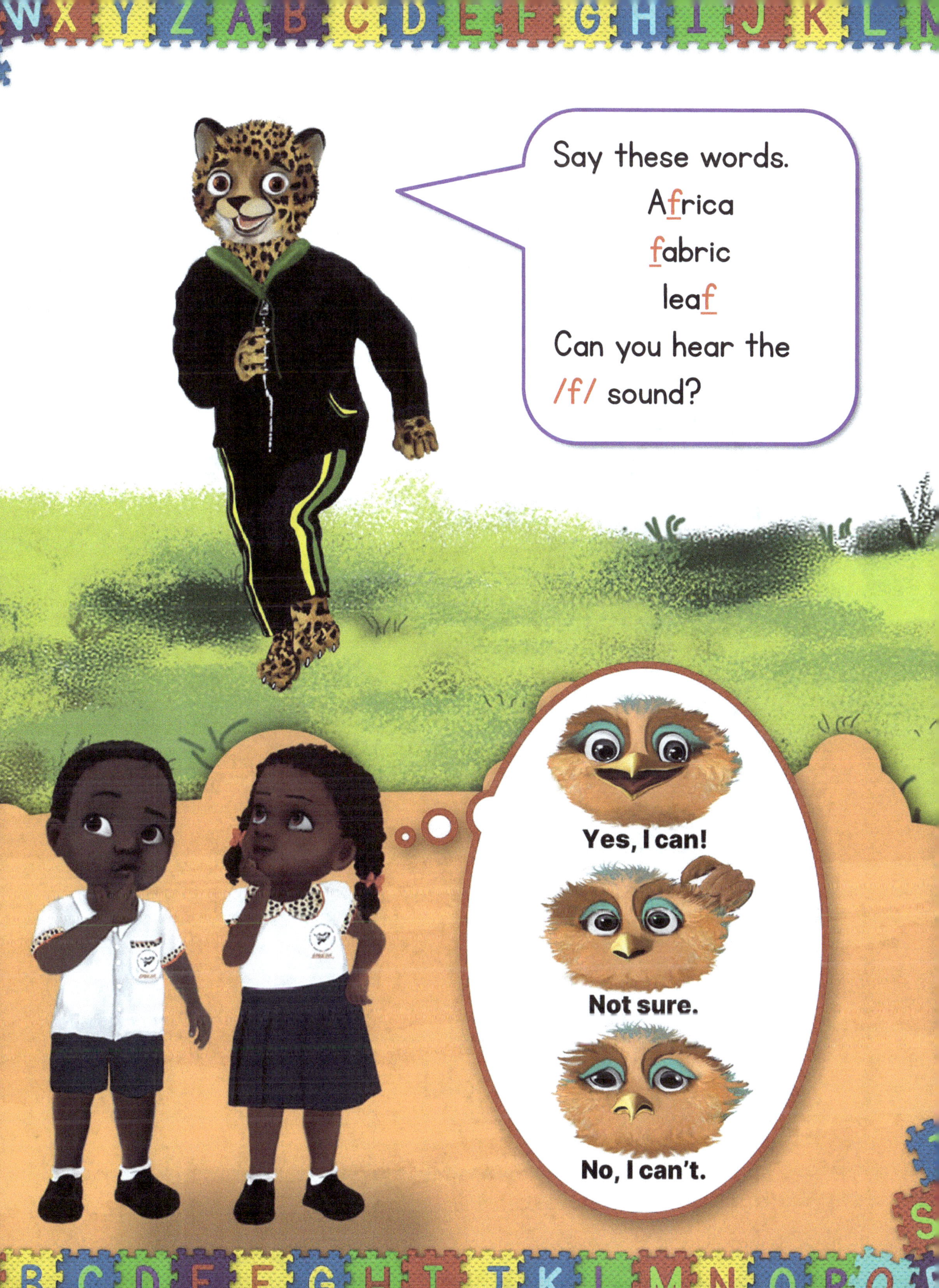
Say these words.
Africa
fabric
leaf
Can you hear the /f/ sound?
Yes, I can!
Not sure.
No, I can't.

Term 2 | hard /g/ sound: initial, medial and final positions

Gg

gold

hard /g/ sound

1. Say my name. Point to each picture. Say its name.

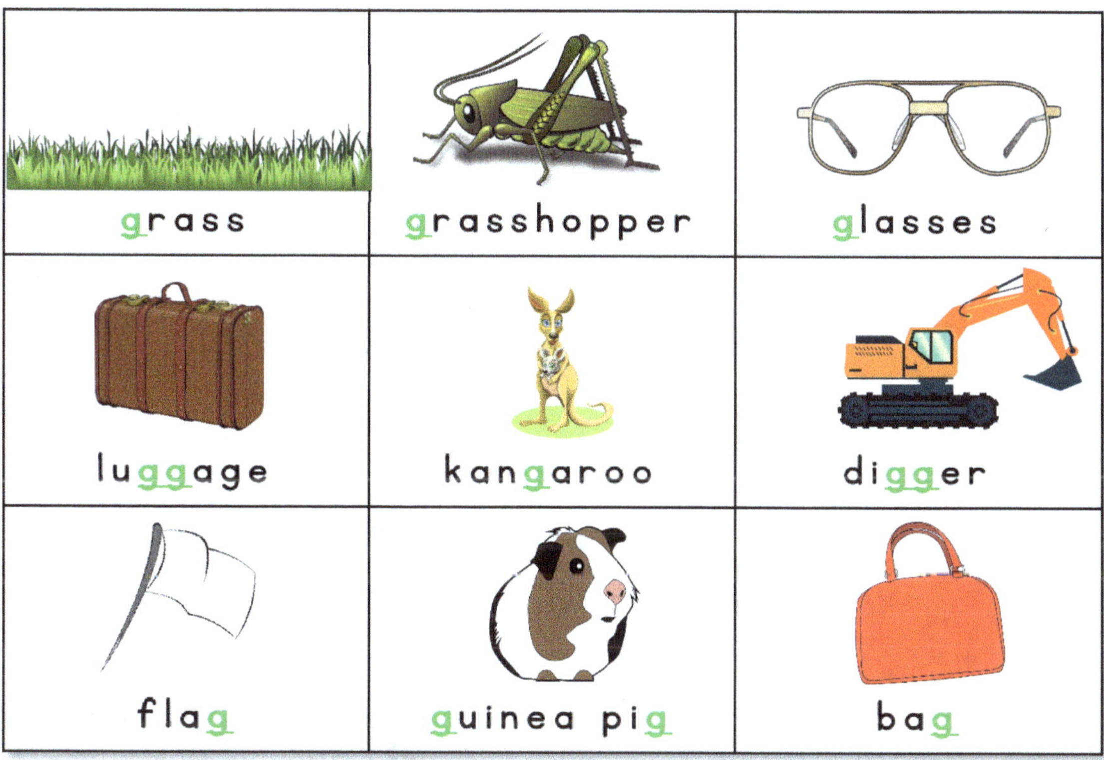

2. Find my letters. Circle the letters then write the name.

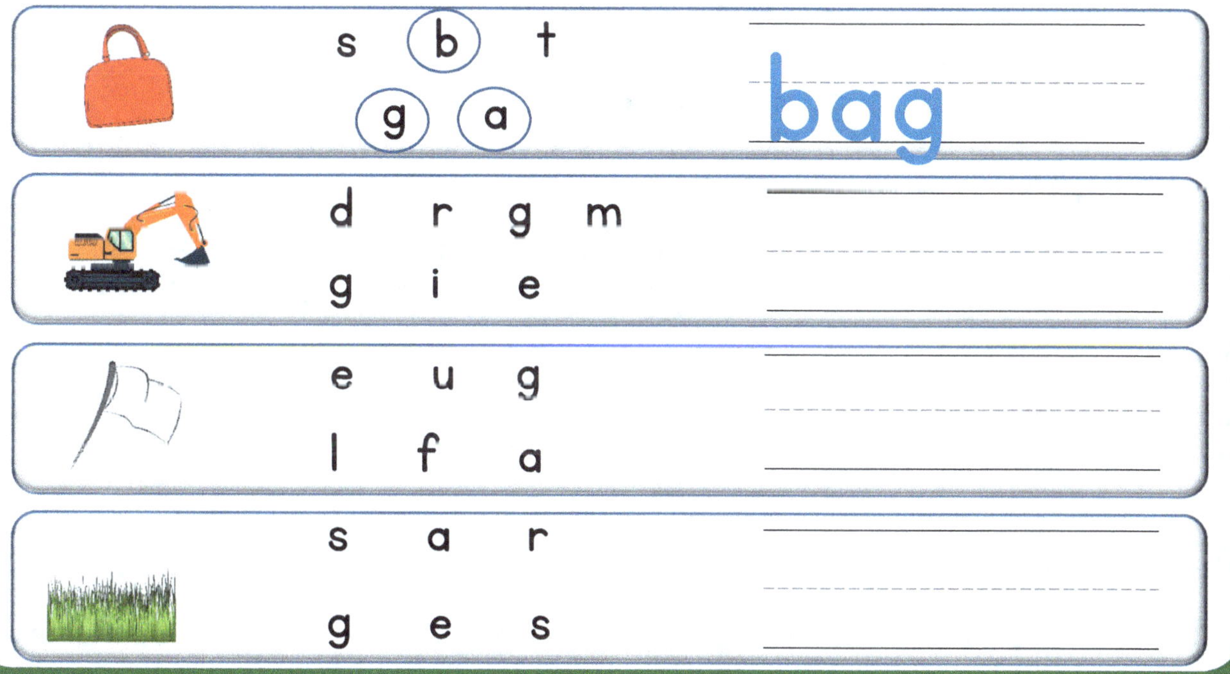

3. Match me. Fill in the missing letter. Match the picture and its name.

lasses

fla

lu**gg**age

kan aroo

4. Find my name. Say the word. Write its name.

Word bank   bag   guinea pig   grasshopper

guinea pig

5. Check me. Look at the picture. Check the name. Write the name.

☐ **g**rass ☑ **g**lasses ☐ **g**uinea pi**g**

glasses

☐ di**gg**er ☐ fla**g** ☐ **g**rasshopper

☐ lu**gg**age ☐ ba**g** ☐ **k**angaroo

6. Read me. Read the sentence.

The **g**rasshopper is on

the lu**gg**age in the **g**rass.

hard /g/ sound

Story words: bag, flag, glasses, grass, grasshopper, guinea pig, kangaroo, luggage

7. Read my story. Look at the pictures. Read the story.

Grasshopper and his friend Guinea Pig are playing in the grass.

They bump into Kangaroo who has luggage and a green bag.

"What do you have?" asks Grasshopper. "A flag? Glasses?"

Kangaroo picks up a book with purple pages and shows his friends.

Say these words.
gold
bingo
bag
Can you hear the /g/ sound?
Yes, I can!
Not sure.
No, I can't.

Term 2

/h/ sound in the initial position

Hh

helicopter
hot air balloon

hot air balloon

/h/ sound

1. **Say my name.** Point to each picture. Say its name.

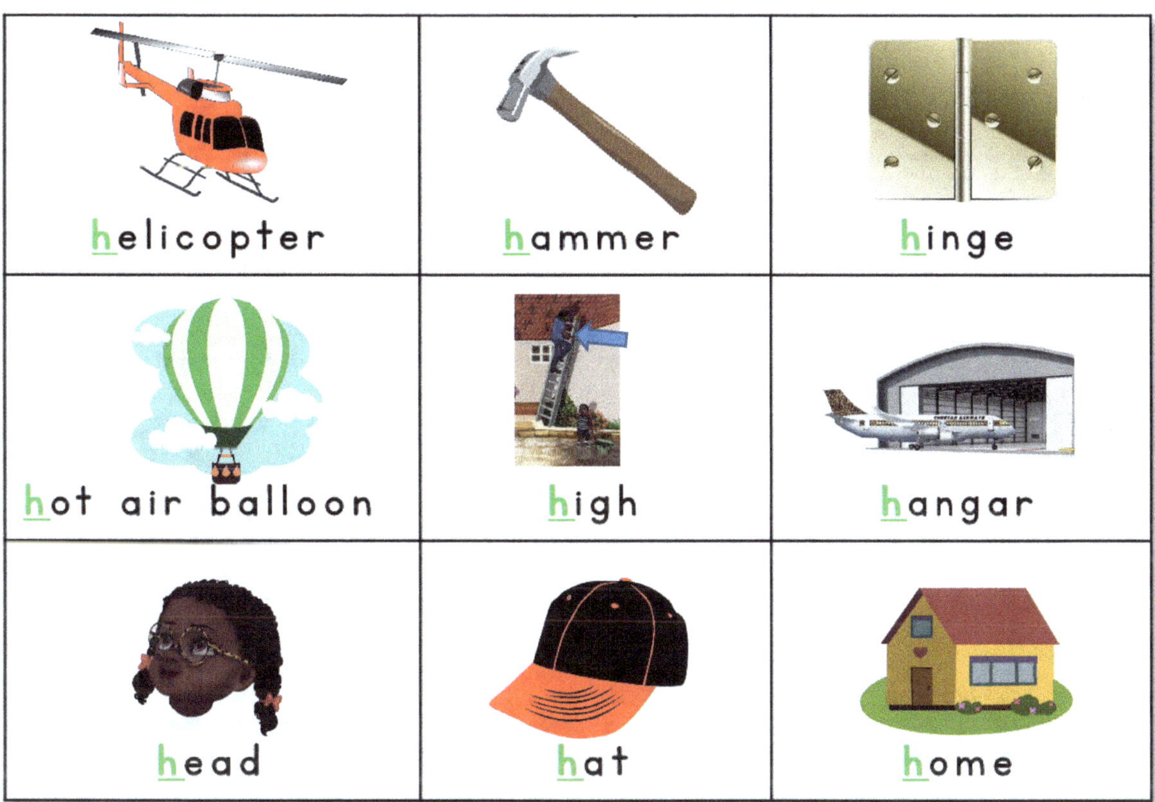

helicopter	**h**ammer	**h**inge
hot air balloon	**h**igh	**h**angar
head	**h**at	**h**ome

2. **Find my name.** Say the word. Write its name.

Word bank

hot air balloon	high	home

high

/h/ sound

3. **Circle my name**. Circle the name of the picture.

(helicopter)   hangar   hammer   head

high   helicopter   hot air balloon   hat

hinge   hangar   head   hammer

head   high   home   hat

4. **Add my letter**. Write the word. Circle the picture.

hat

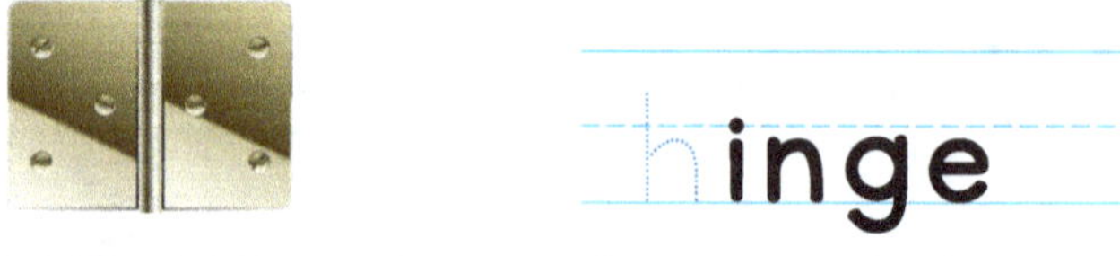

hinge

hammer

/h/ sound

5. Unscramble me. Look at the picture. Unscramble the word to form its name.

a t h      hat

r m h a m e   

a d e h

6. Read me. Read the sentence.

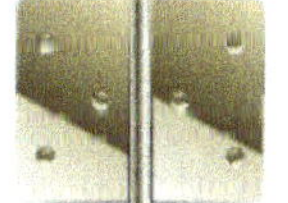

Put the **h**inge on the

helicopter in the **h**angar.

Story words: hammer, helicopter, high, hinge, hot air balloon

7. Read my story. Look at the pictures. Read the story.

A red, white and green hot air balloon flies high in the sky.

Harry lands his hot air balloon. He is there to fix the helicopter.

He takes out his hammer and fixes the hinge on the door.

Then he takes off again in his hot air balloon.

Say these words.
hammer
helicopter
hot air balloon
Can you hear the /h/ sound?
Yes, I can!
Not sure.
No, I can't.

Sub-theme: Our people from India

Term 1 — short /i/ sound: initial, medial and final positions

Ii

India
Singh
Divali

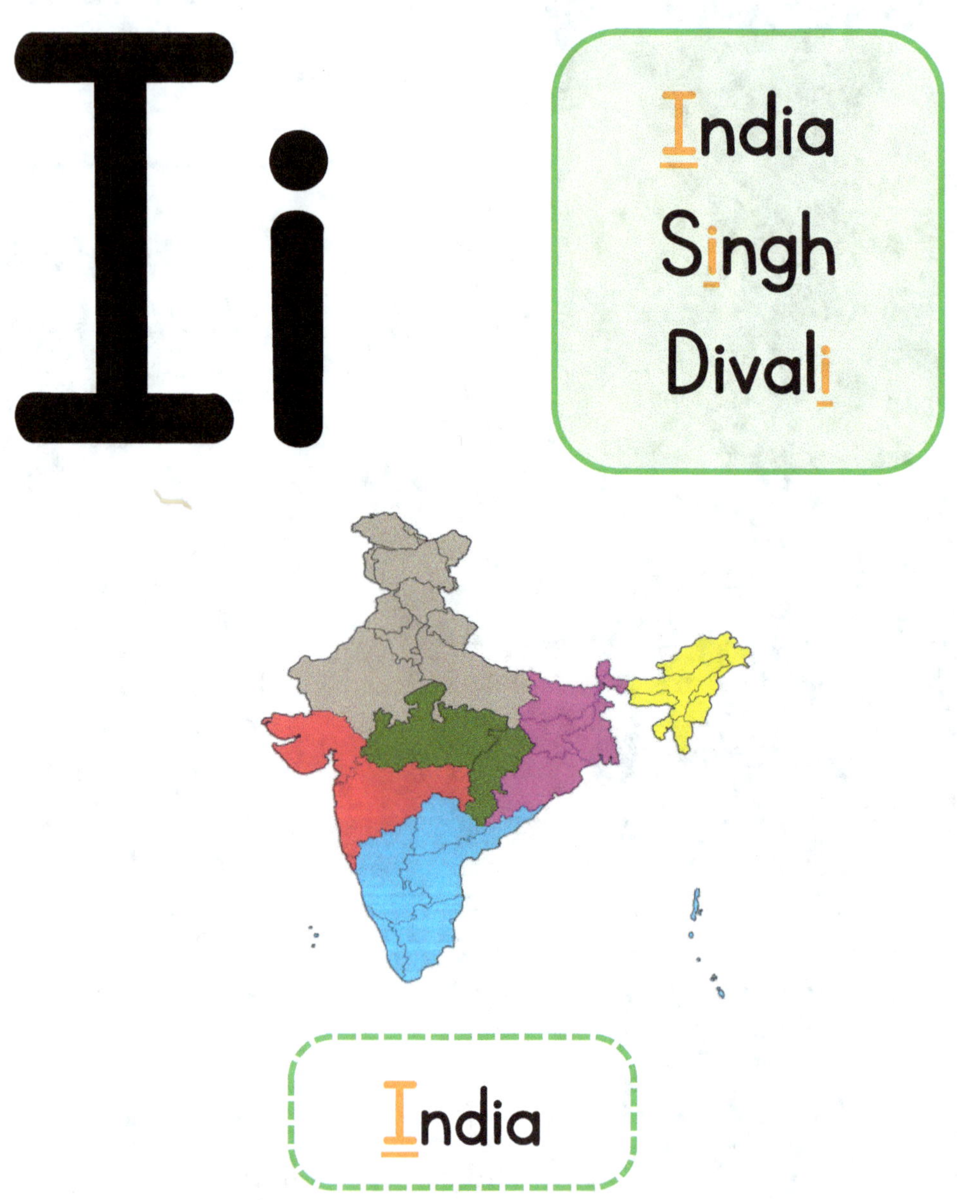

India

short /i/ sound

1. Say my name. Point to each picture. Say its name.

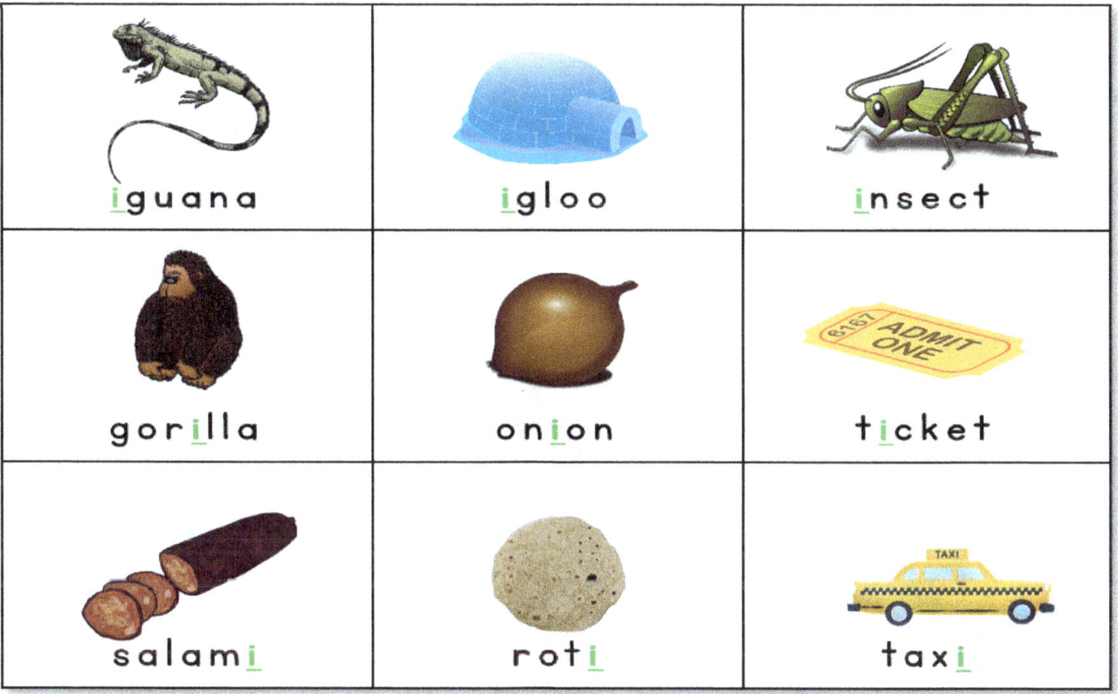

2. Add my letter. Write the word. Circle the picture.

3. Trace my name. Circle the picture. Trace its name.

   iguana

   ticket

   salami

4. Write my name. Write the name in the sentence.

The _taxi_ is yellow. 

Will the __________ jump? 

I like __________ . 

short /i/ sound

5. Check me. Look at the picture. Check the name. Write the name.

☐ gor_i_lla   ☑ _i_gloo   ☐ on_i_on

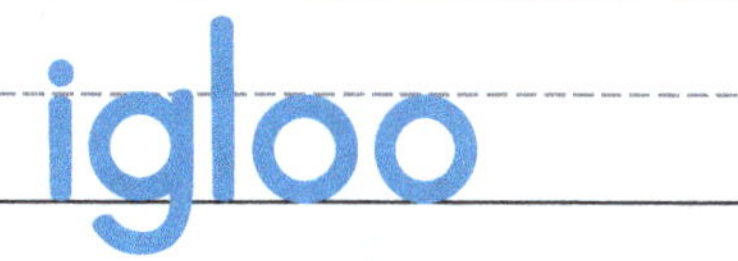

☐ salam_i_   ☐ rot_i_   ☐ _i_guana

☐ tax_i_   ☐ _i_nsect   ☐ t_i_cket

6. Read me. Read the sentence.

The gor_i_lla took the tax_i_ to the _i_gloo.

Story words: igloo, iguana, insect, onion, roti, salami, taxi

7. Read my story. Look at the pictures. Read the story.

Indie, the insect, drinks juice from his igloo as Iggie, the iguana cooks.

Iggie is cooking salami and roti. He chops a big onion with a knife.

The onion makes his eyes water. He cannot see the food and he burns it.

So, they take his taxi to a restaurant.

Say these words.
India
Singh
Divali
Can you hear the /i/ sound?
Yes, I can!
Not sure.
No, I can't.

Jj

jewellery

/j/ sound

1. Say my name. Point to each picture. Say its name.

jacks	**j**eans	**j**ewellery
jelly	**j**ackal	**j**igsaw
ob**j**ect	py**j**amas	en**j**oy

2. Find my name. Say the word. Write its name.

Word bank	
enjoy jigsaw jeans	

jigsaw

____

____

/j/ sound

3. Check me. Look at the picture. Check the name. Write the name.

☐ jelly ☑ jewellery ☐ jeans

jewellery

☐ enjoy ☐ pyjamas ☐ object

☐ jigsaw ☐ jacks ☐ jackal

4. Read me. Read the sentence.

I see a jackal wearing pyjamas and eating jelly. 

/j/ sound

5. Circle my name. Circle the name of the picture.

 jelly   jackal   (jigsaw)   jeans

 jelly   jacks   object   jewellery

 jackal   enjoy   pyjamas   jigsaw

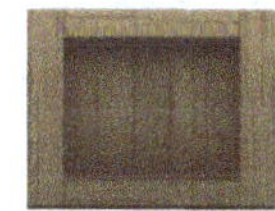 jacks   jeans   object   jelly

6. Find my letters. Circle the letters then write the name.

   (k) (s) m   (j) (c) (a)   **jacks**

   o t b f   j c y e

    y l t   l e j

   s j e   p n a

/j/ sound

Story words: jacks, jeans, jewellery, jelly, jackal, jigsaw, object, pyjamas, enjoy

7. Read my story. Look at the pictures. Read the story.

Jackie the jackal has a fun day.

She plays jacks. She makes jewellery with colourful objects. She does jigsaw puzzles.

Time to enjoy some jelly.

Poor Jackie is sleepy. She takes off her jeans and puts on her pyjamas.

Goodnight, Jackie. Sweet dreams.

Say this word.
jelly
jewellery
enjoy
Can you hear the /j/ sound?
Yes, I can!
Not sure.
No, I can't.

Kk

kayak

/k/ sound

1. Say my name. Point to each picture. Say its name.

kayak	**k**iwi	**k**oala
bi**k**e	coo**k**ie	don**k**ey
duc**k**	boo**k**	for**k**

2. Find my name. Say the word. Write its name.

Word bank

koala	kayak	duck

duck

/k/ sound

3. **Add my letter**. Write the word. Circle the picture.

cookie
cookie

donkey

book

4. **Find my letters**. Circle the letters then write the name.

i w p
k m i

kiwi

a i e
k c b

b k g
o f o

f t o
k h r

/k/ sound

5. Unscramble me. Look at the picture. Unscramble the word to form its name.

i k b e  bike

a y k a k 

o f k r

6. Read me. Read the sentence.

The **k**oala ate the coo**k**ie

with a for**k**.

/k/ sound

Story words: bike, book, cookie, donkey, duck, fork, kayak, kiwi, koala

7. Read my story. Look at the pictures. Read the story.

1

Koala rides her bike to the big lake to meet her friend, Donkey.

2

They go for a ride in a kayak. See the duck splashing in the water!

3

For lunch, they eat green kiwi. Donkey uses a fork. They share a cookie for dessert.

4

Then they read a book. Soon it is time to go home. What a great day!

Say this word.
bike
book
kayak
Can you hear the /k/ sound?
Yes, I can!
Not sure.
No, I can't.

Theme: Transportation

Sub-theme: Types of air transportation

Term 2

/l/ sound: initial, medial and final positions

Ll

low
plane
tail

plane

/l/ sound

1. Say my name. Point to each picture. Say its name.

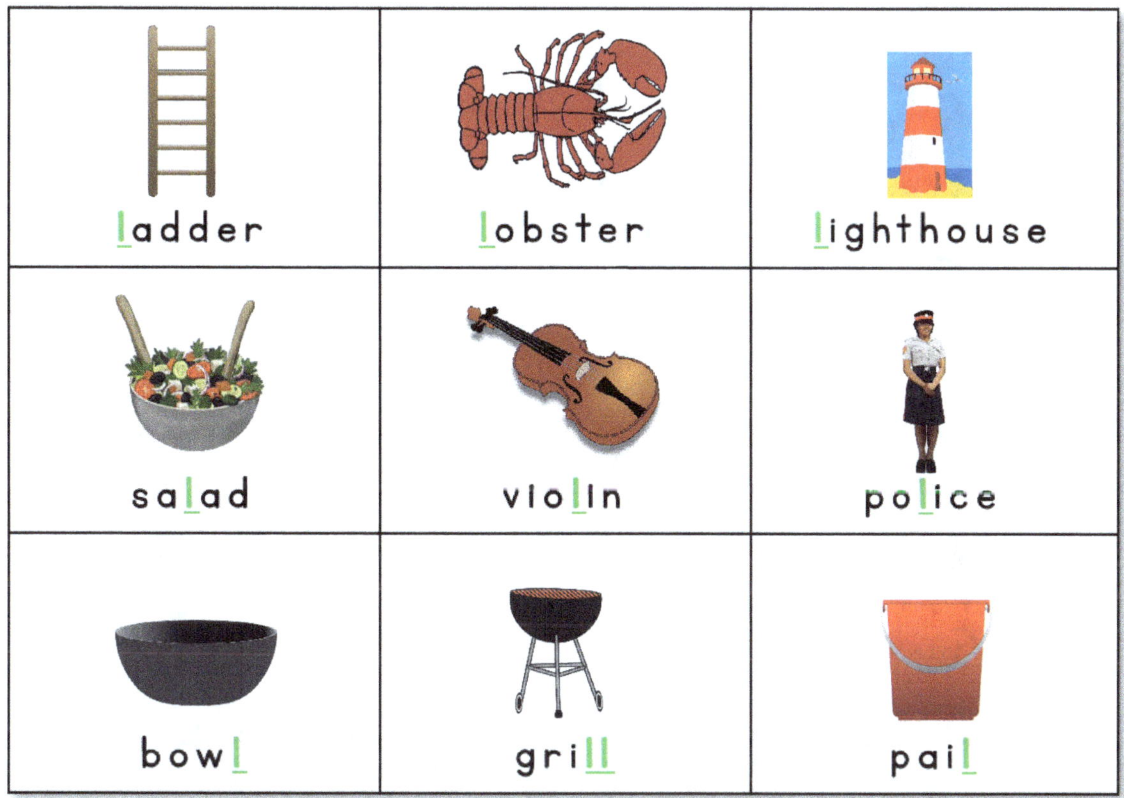

ladder	lobster	lighthouse
salad	violin	police
bowl	grill	pail

2. Circle my name. Circle the name of the picture.

(lighthouse)   police   grill   lobster

ladder   violin   salad   bowl

salad   ladder   lobster   pail

police   grill   lighthouse   violin

/l/ sound

3. Add my letter. Write the word. Circle the picture.

 ladder
ladder

 pail

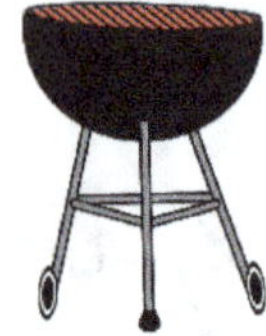 gril

4. Match me. Fill in the missing letter. Match the picture and its name.

adder

bow

violin

po ice

/l/ sound

5. **Check me**. Look at the picture. Check the name. Write the name.

☐ _l_obster   ☑ _l_ighthouse   ☐ pai_l_

lighthouse

☐ bow_l_   ☐ _l_adder   ☐ sa_l_ad

☐ vio_l_in   ☐ gri_ll_   ☐ po_l_ice

6. **Read me**. Read the sentence.

Put the _l_obster in the pai_l_

with the sa_l_ad.

/l/ sound

Story words: bowl, grill, ladder, pail, lighthouse, lobster, police, salad, violin

7. **Read my story.** Look at the pictures. Read the story.

1 

A man lives in a lighthouse. He lost his violin and his pail.

2 

He is hungry. He puts lobster on the grill and a bowl of salad on the table.

3 

The doorbell rings. He climbs down the ladder and sees the police at the door.

4 

He smiles. She has his missing violin and his pail.

W X Y Z A B C D E F G H I J K L M

Say these words.
low
plane
tail
Can you hear the /l/ sound?

Yes, I can!
Not sure.
No, I can't.

B C D E F G H I J K L M N O P Q
S

Term 1

/m/ sound: initial, medial and final positions

Mm

tamarind

/m/ sound

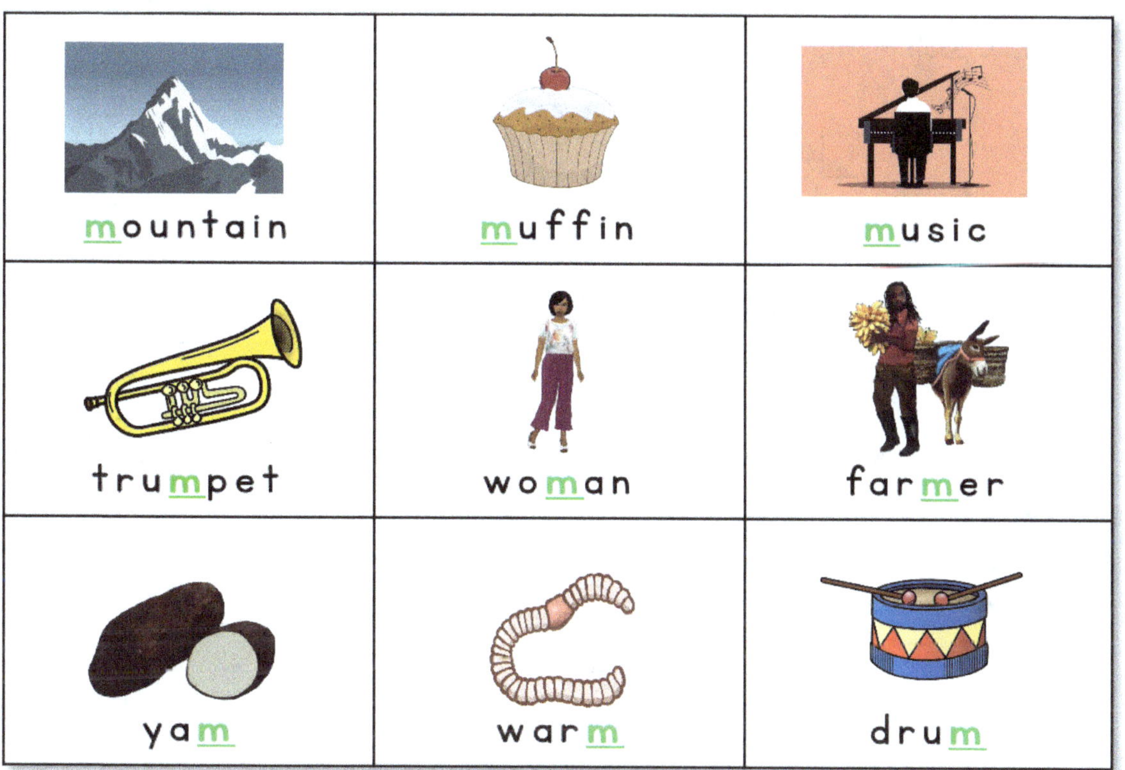

2. **Match me**. Fill in the missing letter. Match the picture and its name.

3. **Check me**. Look at the picture. Check the name. Write the name.

☐ **m**usic   ☐ ya**m**   ☑ wo**m**an

woman

☐ far**m**er   ☐ tru**m**pet   ☐ dru**m**

☐ **m**uffin   ☐ **m**ountain   ☐ wor**m**

4. **Read me**. Read the sentence.

Use the dru**m** and the

tru**m**pet to make **m**usic.

/m/ sound

5. Add my letter. Write the word. Circle the picture.

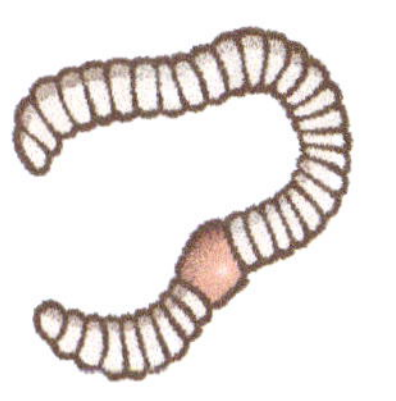

music

music

farmer

yam

6. Write my name. Write the name in the sentence.

Do you want a muffin.

The ___________ is loud.

See the ___________ .

/m/ sound

Story words: drum, farmer, mountain, muffins, music, trumpet, woman, worms, yam

7. **Read my story**. Look at the pictures. Read the story.

The farmer and the old woman live on a mountain.

Every morning, they play music for their neighbours. He plays the trumpet. She plays the drum.

In the evening, the farmer digs yam for dinner. Oh no! It has worms!

They will eat cinnamon muffins instead.

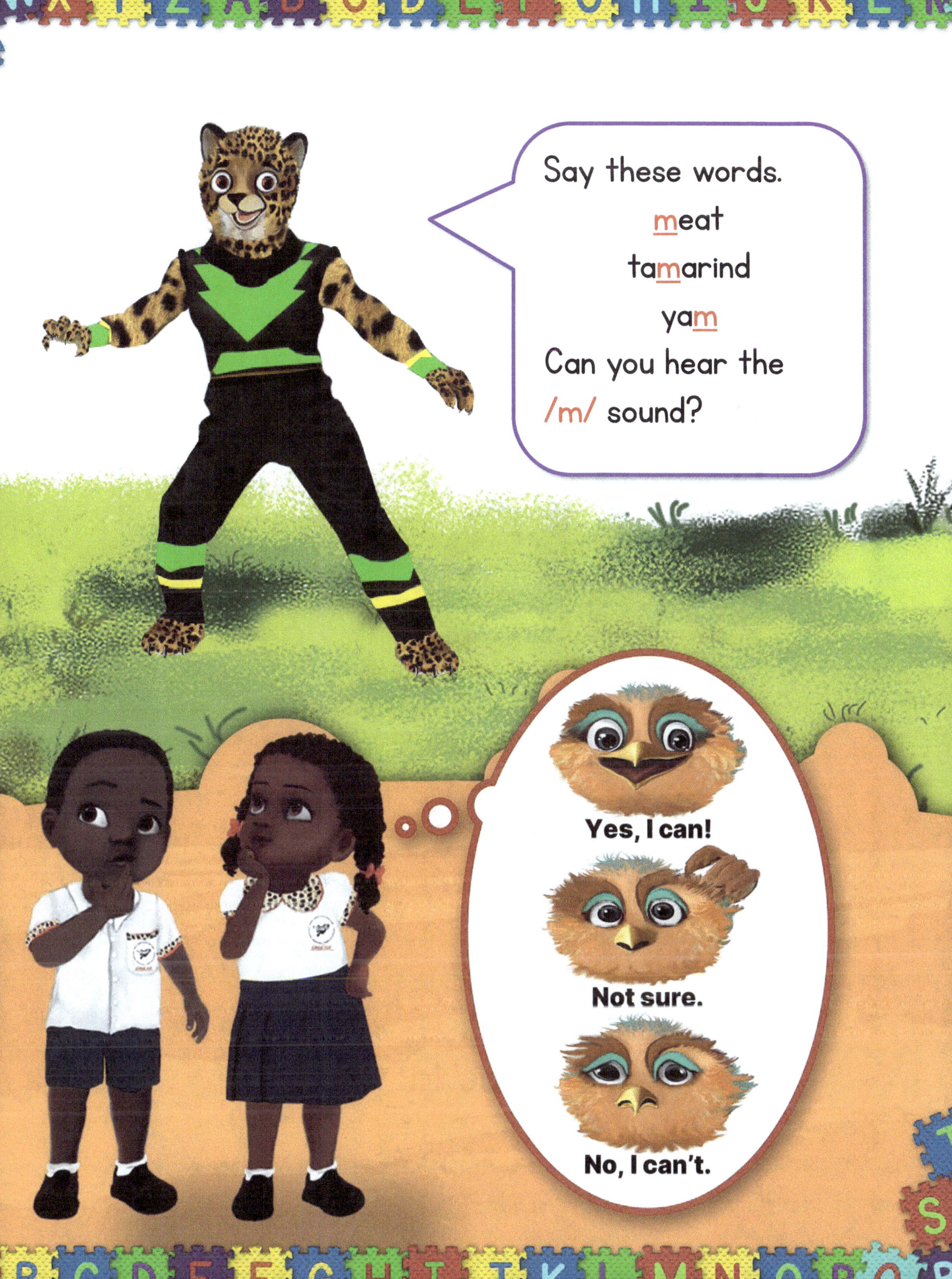

Say these words.
meat
tamarind
yam
Can you hear the
/m/ sound?
Yes, I can!
Not sure.
No, I can't.

Term 1

/n/ sound: initial, medial and final positions

Nn

fa**n**
napkin
Chi**n**ese
la**n**tern

Chi**n**ese la**n**tern

/n/ sound

1. **Say my name.** Point to each picture. Say its name.

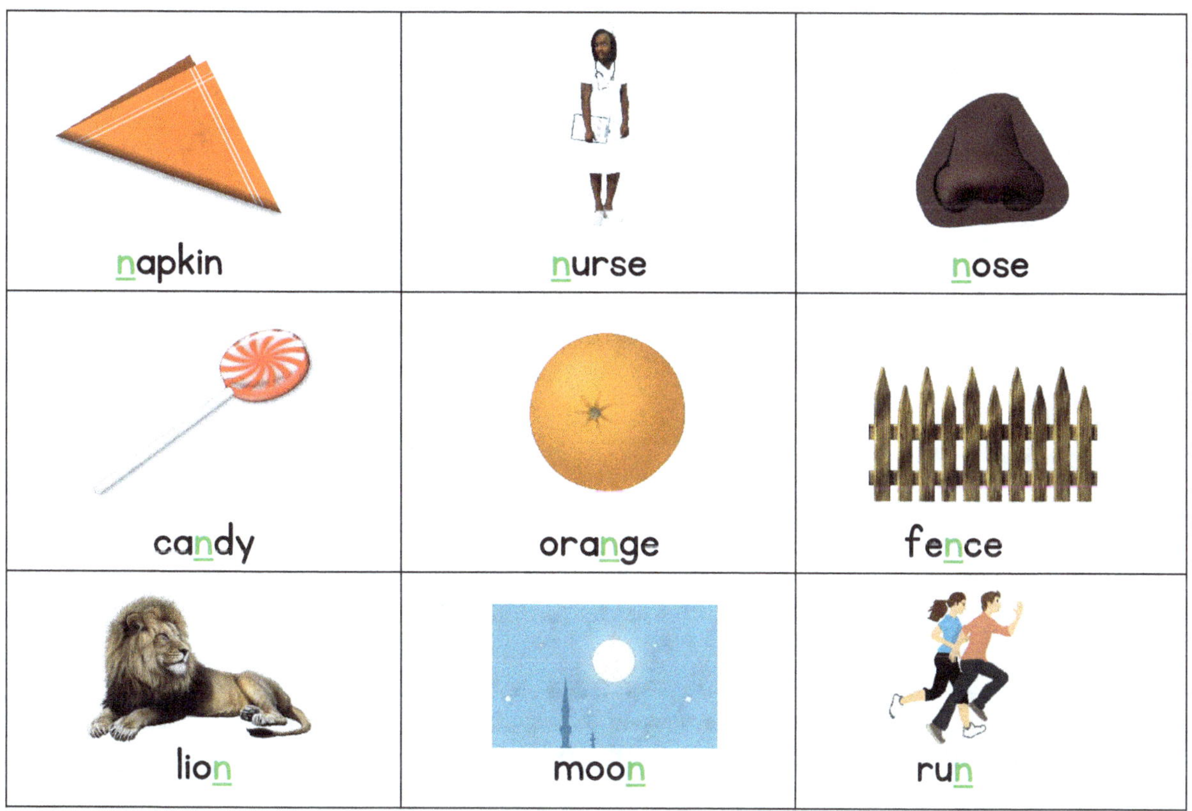

2. **Circle my name.** Circle the name of the picture.

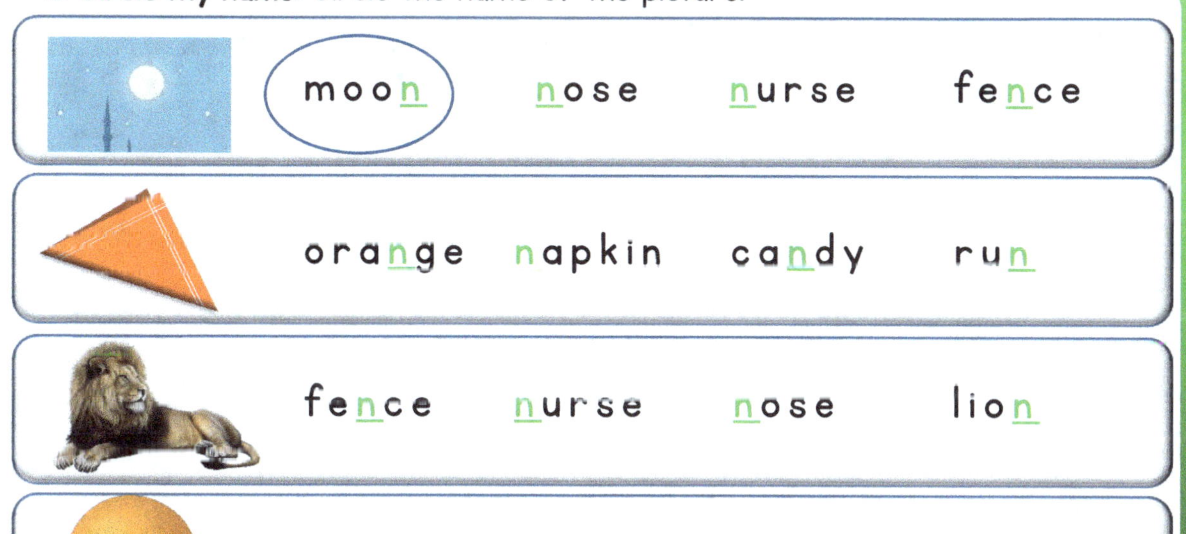

/n/ sound

3. **Match me**. Fill in the missing letter. Match the picture and its name.

ca_dy

run

_urse

fe_ce

4. **Trace my name**. Circle the picture. Trace its name.

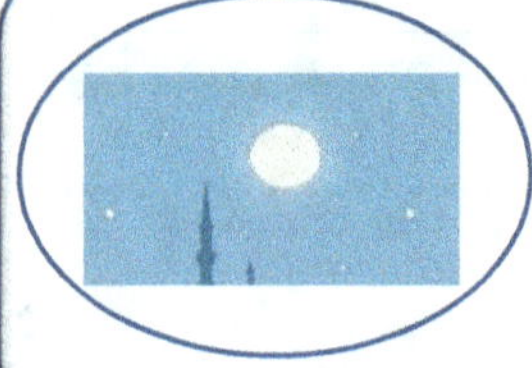 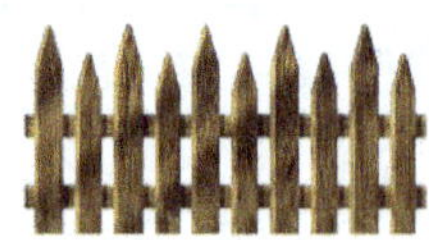 

moon

napkin

nose

5. **Unscramble me**. Look at the picture. Unscramble the word to form its name.

i n o l

lion

n a r e o g

s e n r u

6. **Read me**. Read the sentence.

Ru<u>n</u> to the fe<u>n</u>ce and look

at the moo<u>n</u>.

/n/ sound

7. Read my story. Look at the pictures. Read the story.

1

Look at the lion run!

2

Can he jump over the moon?

3

Oh, no! He falls and bumps his nose.

4

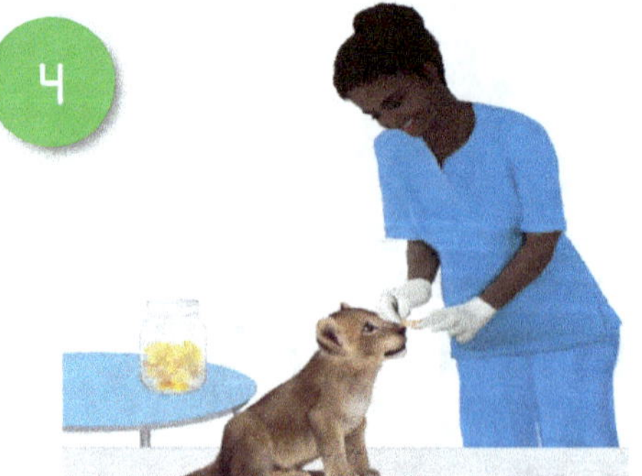

He goes to the nurse. She wipes his nose with a napkin and gives him orange candy.

5

Look at the lion run! He can jump over the fence.

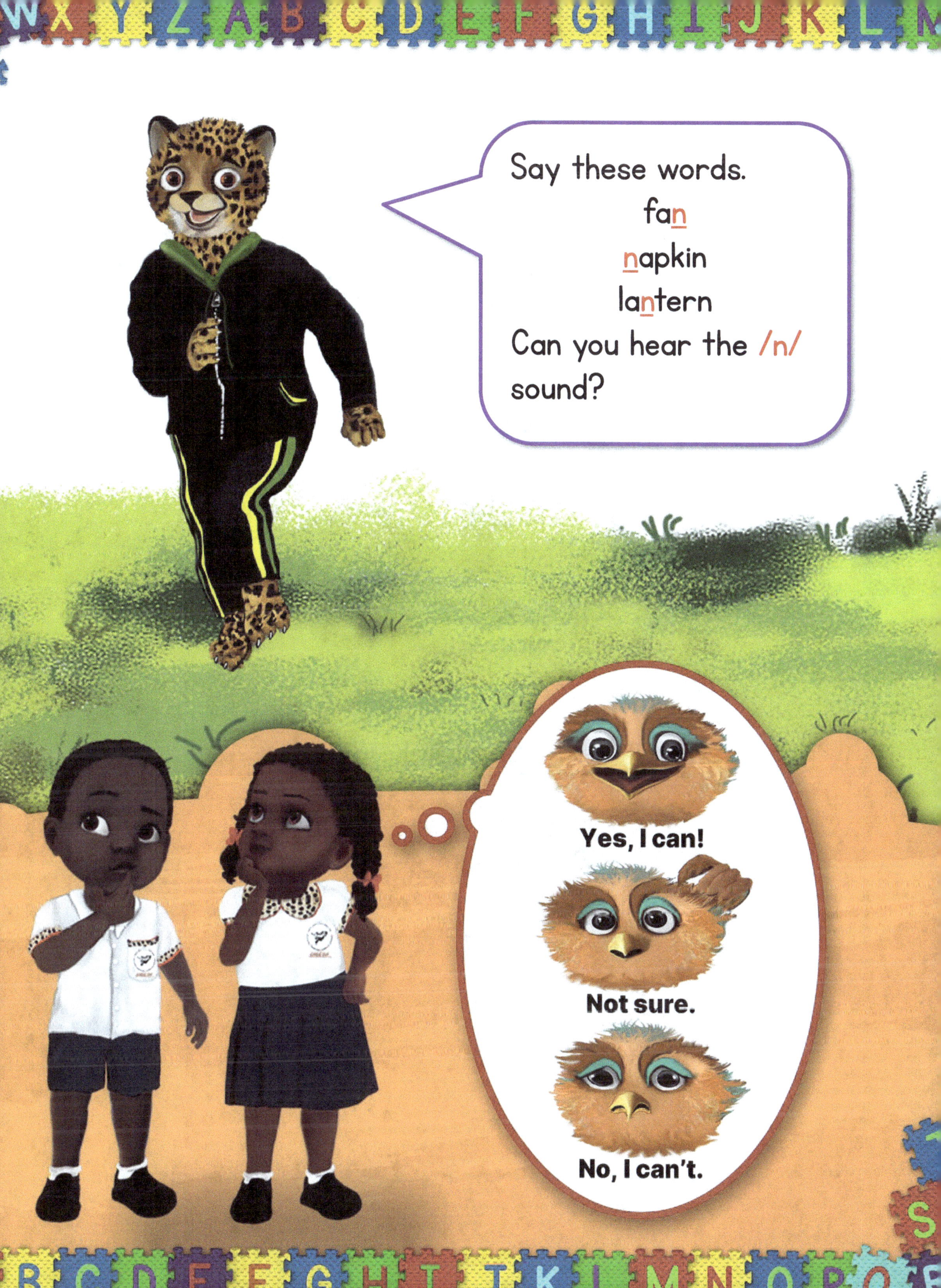

Say these words.
fan
napkin
lantern
Can you hear the /n/ sound?
Yes, I can!
Not sure.
No, I can't.

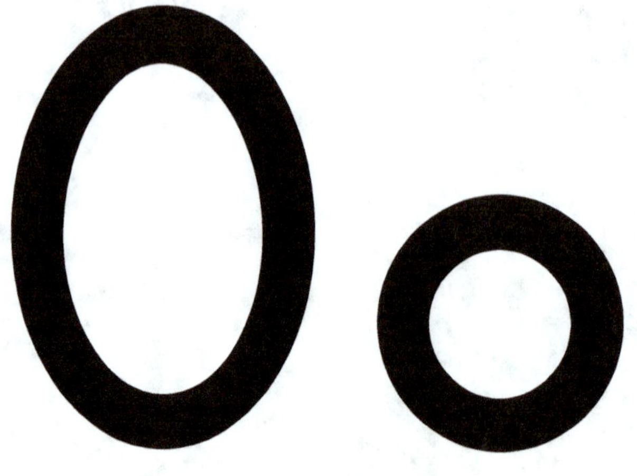

ox

short /o/ sound

1. **Say my name.** Point to each picture. Say its name.

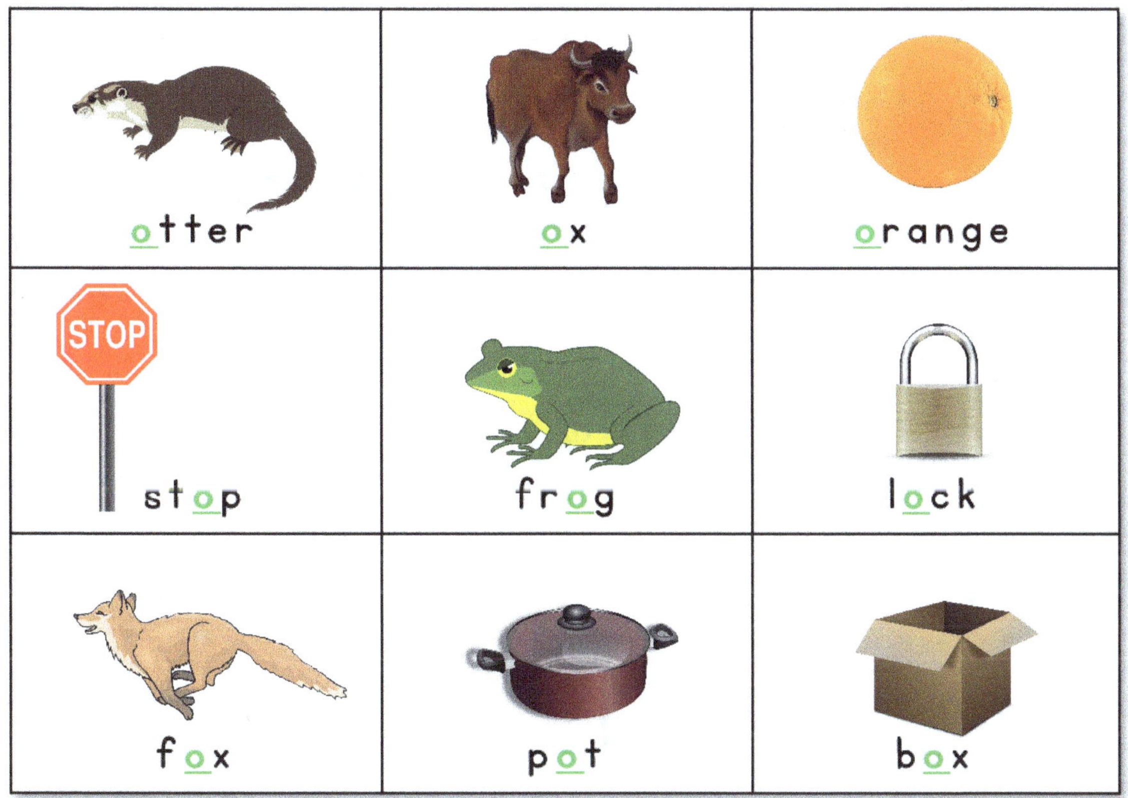

2. **Match my parts.** Circle the parts to make the name.

short /o/ sound

3. Trace my name. Circle the picture. Trace its name.

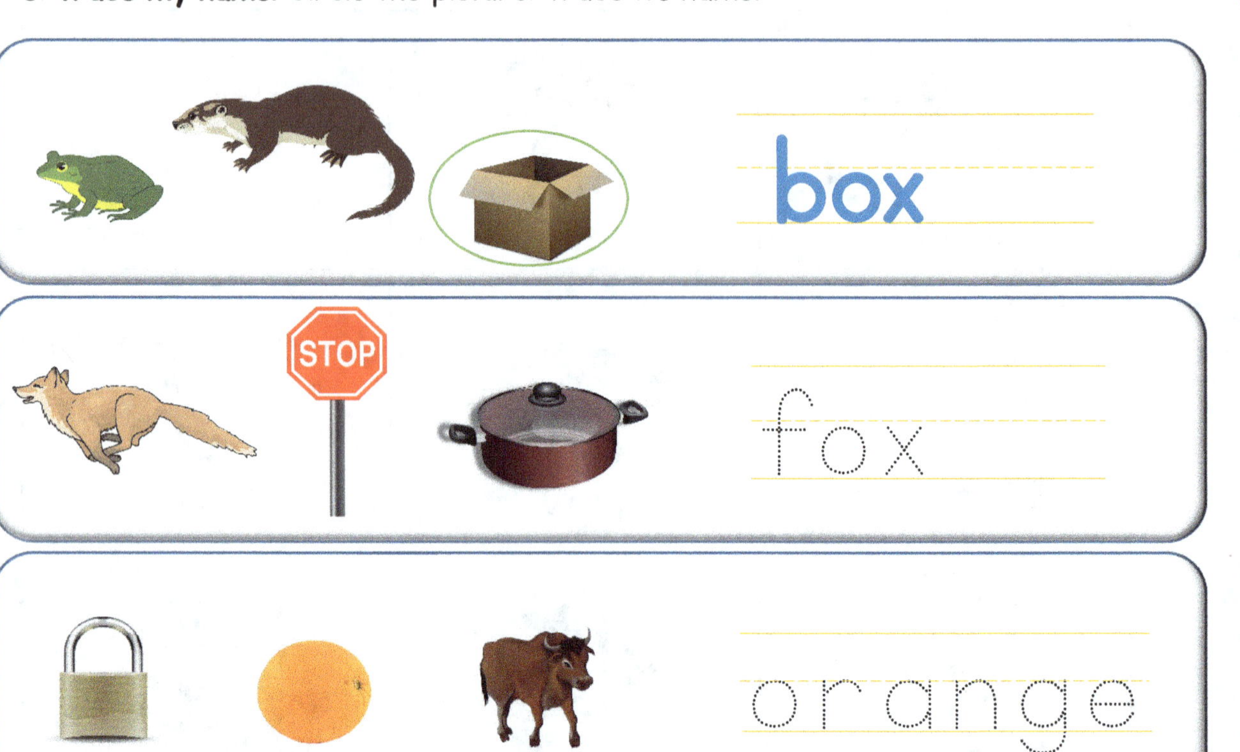

4. Find my name. Say the word. Write its name.

Word bank

otter   ox   pot

pot

short /o/ sound

5. Circle then write my name. Look at the picture. Circle its name. Write its name.

st**o**p

p**o**t

stop

l**o**ck

orange

otter

f**o**x

6. Read me. Read the sentence.

Put the l**o**ck and the p**o**t

in the b**o**x.

short /o/ sound

Story words: box, fox, frog, locks, oranges, otter, ox, pot

7. **Read my story**. Look at the pictures. Read the story.

Ox loves oranges.

His friend, Otter, stops by and gives him a box full.

Ox sees greedy Fox and Frog coming.

Ox knows they will eat all his oranges, so he hides the box.

Then Otter says, 'No, share.'

So, Ox locks a few in a pot instead.

Say this word.
ox
lock
pot
Can you hear the /o/ sound?
Yes, I can!
Not sure.
No, I can't.

Sub-theme: What is the weather like?

Term 3 | long /o/ sound: ō. Extended learning: oa, a_e (vcv)

long o

cold

long /ō/ sound

1. Say my name. Point to each picture. Say its name.

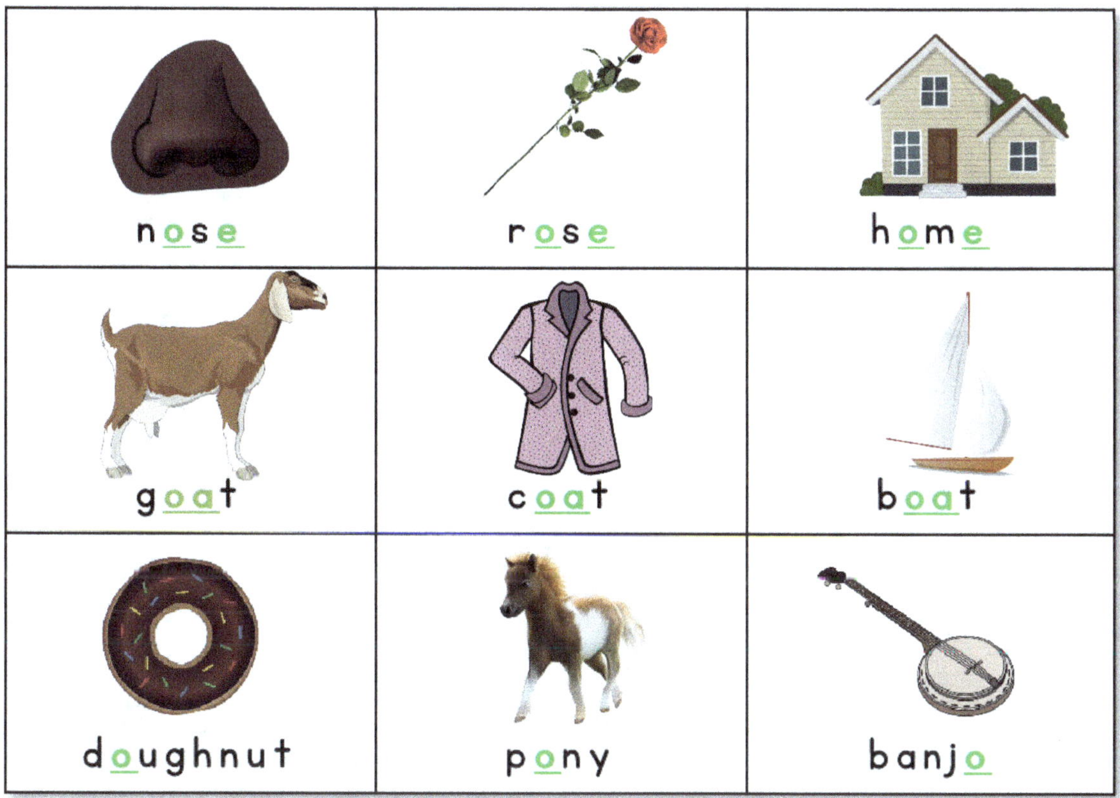

2. Match me. Fill in the missing letter. Match the picture and its name.

long /ō/ sound

3. Write my name. Write the name in the sentence.

I like my **home** . 

Eat the __________ . 

Listen to the __________ . 

4. Match my parts. Circle the parts to make the name.

r
o s e
n

b
o a t
g

b
o a t
c

r
o s e
n

long /ō/ sound

5. Circle then write my name. Look at the picture. Circle its name. Write its name.

rose

nose

rose

home

coat

pony

boat

6. Read me. Read the sentence.

The goat gave the doughnut

to the pony.

long /ō/ sound

Story words: banjo, coat, doughnut, goat, home, nose, pony, rose

7. Read my story. Look at the pictures. Read the story.

Goat puts on his red coat. He is going to get doughnuts.

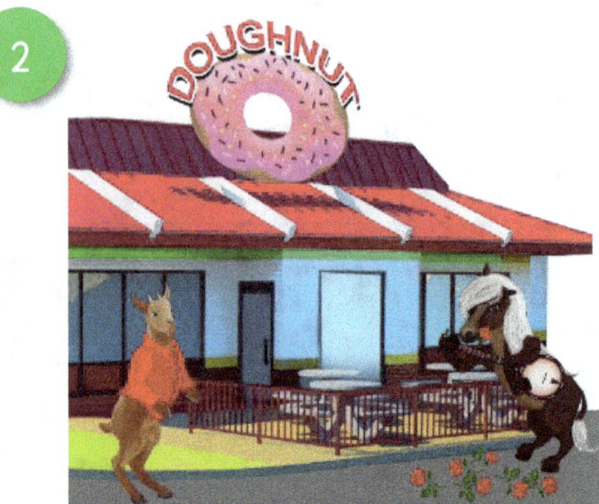

Outside the doughnut shop, he sees a pony playing the banjo.

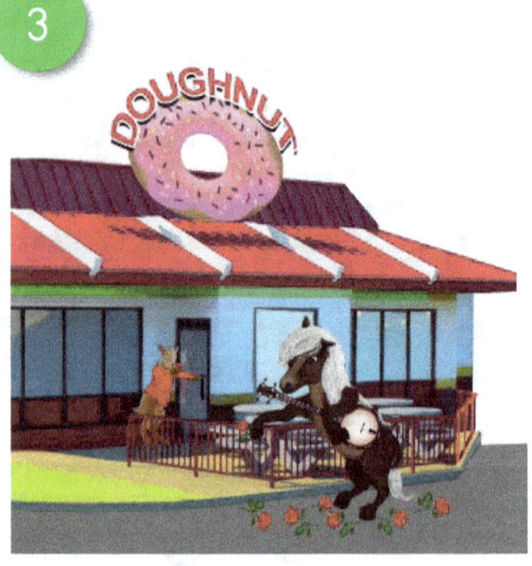

The pony gives him a rose. Goat puts it to his nose. "Ahh!" he says.

Goat goes home with his doughnut and rose. It is a good day.

Say these words.
cold
hello
nose
Can you hear the long o sound?
Yes, I can!
Not sure.
No, I can't.

Term 1

/p/ sound: initial, medial and final positions

Pp

pita

pumpkin

shop

shop

/p/ sound

1. Say my name. Point to each point. Say its name.

pillow	penguin	prize
rope	paper	compass
ship	sleep	clap

2. Circle my name. Circle the name of the picture.

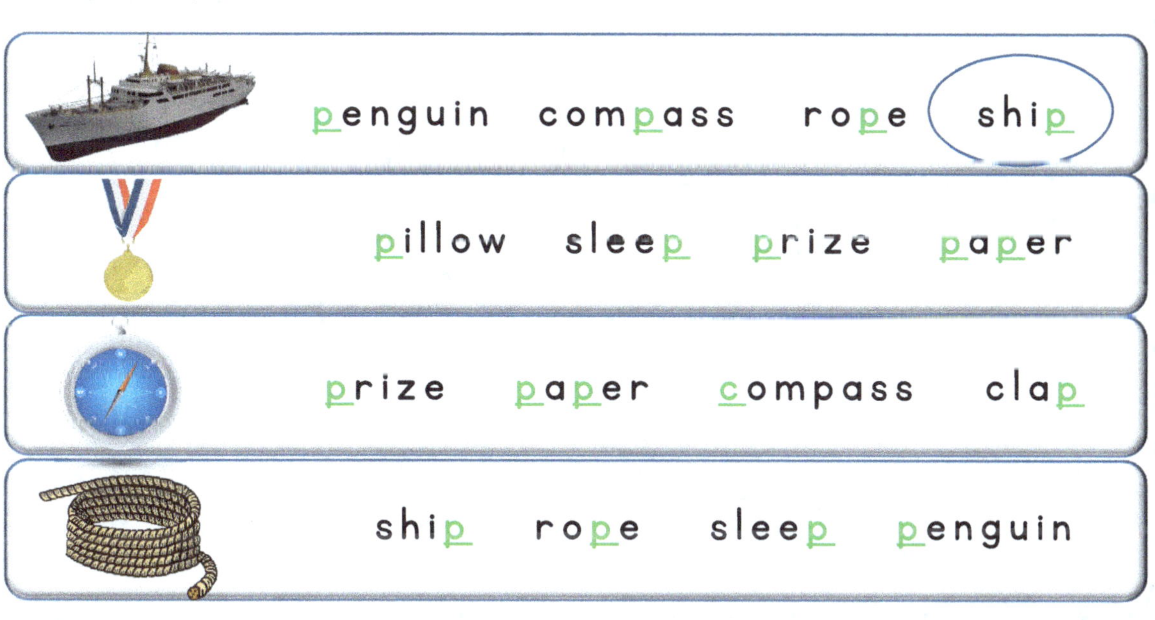

	penguin compass rope (ship)
	pillow sleep prize paper
	prize paper compass clap
	ship rope sleep penguin

/p/ sound

3. Trace my name. Circle the picture. Trace its name.

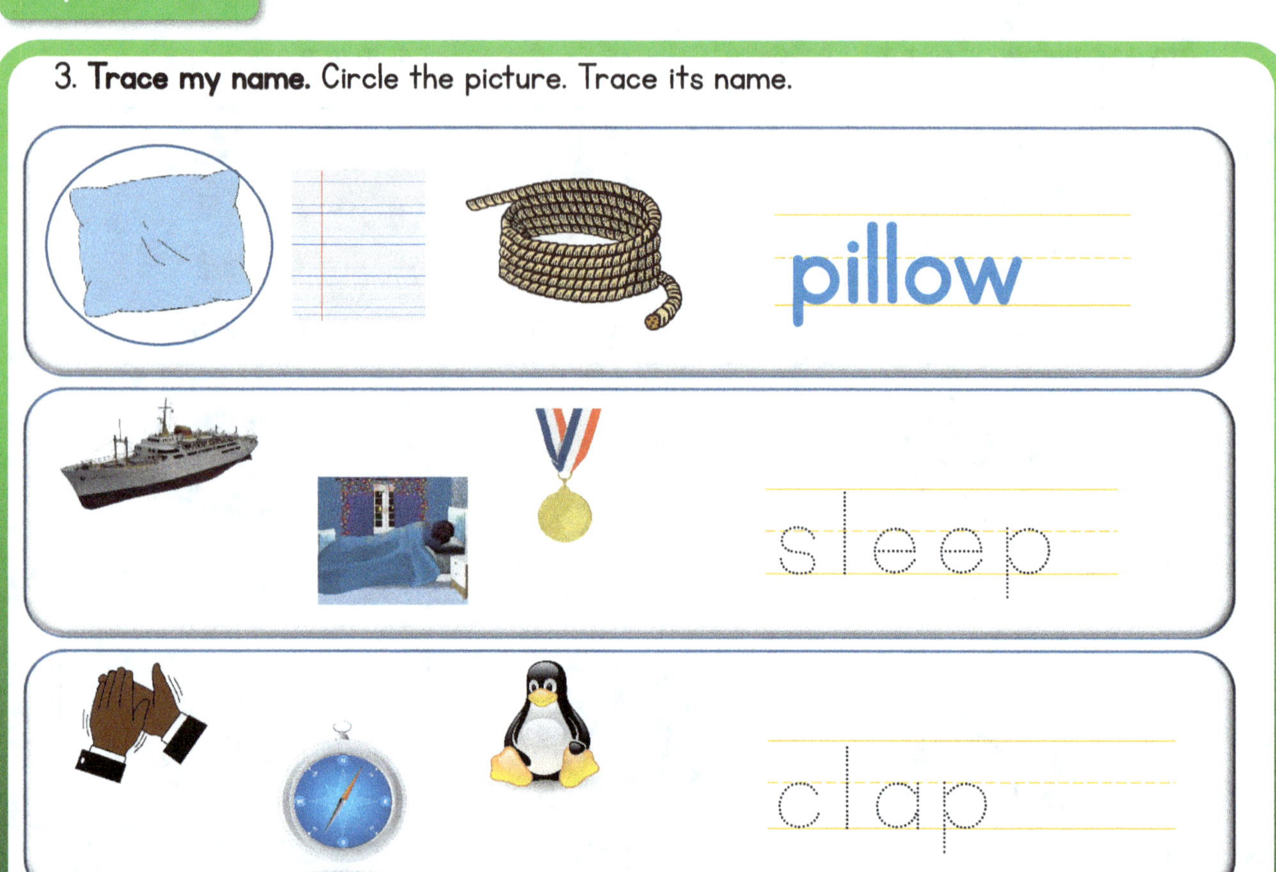

pillow

sleep

clap

4. Find my name. Say the word. Write its name.

Word bank

ship   penguin   paper

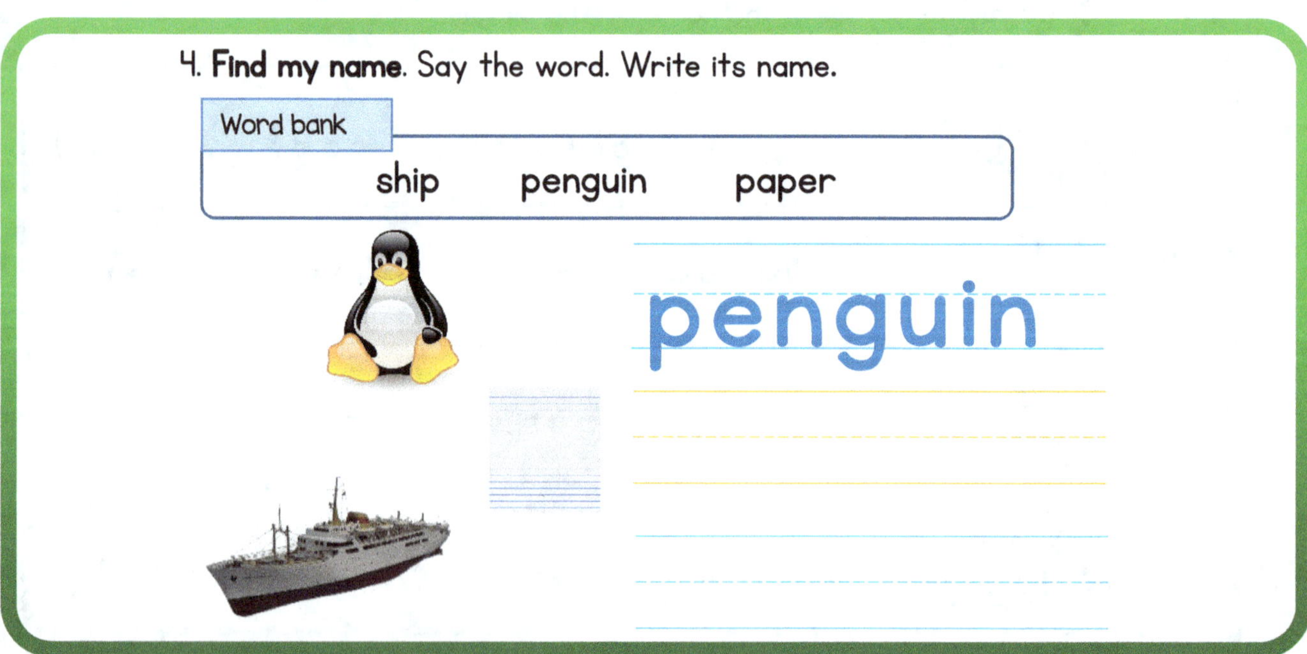

penguin

/p/ sound

5. Circle then write my name. Look at the picture. Circle its name. Write its name.

paper

prize

paper

pillow

clap

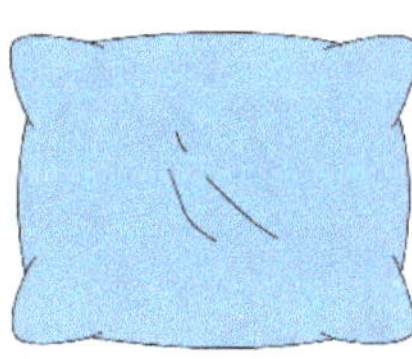

compass

penguin

6. Read me. Read the sentence.

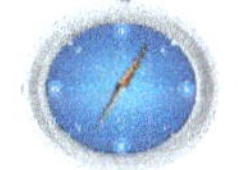

A compass and rope are

used on a ship.

/p/ sound

Story words: clap, compass, paper, penguin, pillow, prize, ship, sleep, stop

7. **Read my story**. Look at the pictures. Read the story.

1

Penguin is on his ship with his compass and paper map.

2

Penguin hopes to win the prize when they stop at the island.

3

He wants to tell Sheep his plans, but Sheep is sleeping on a pillow.

4

Penguin claps his hands to wake him. But Sheep keeps sleeping.

Say these words.
pita
pumpkin
shop
Can you hear the /p/ sound?
Yes, I can!
Not sure.
No, I can't.

Qq

quill

1. Say my name. Point to each picture. Say its name.

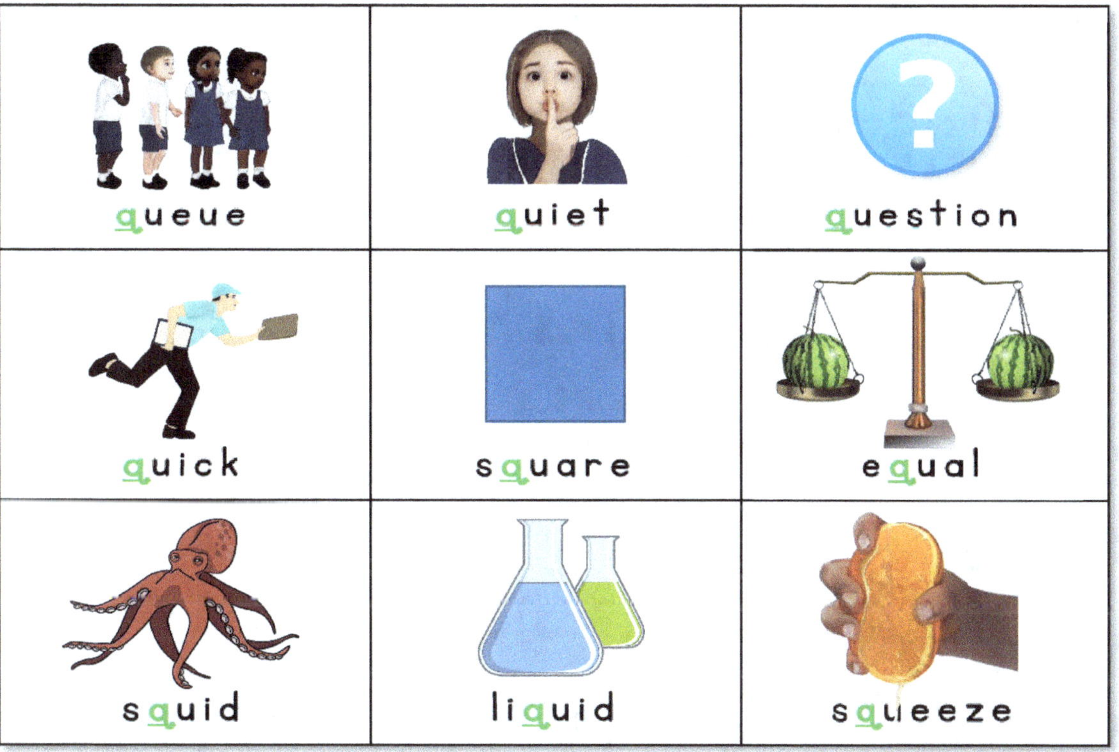

2. Add my letter. Write the word. Circle the picture.

'q' sound /kw/

3. Circle my name. Circle the name of the picture.

(liquid) equal squid squeeze

square question queue quiet

liquid quiet quick question

equal squeeze square squid

4. Write my name. Write the name in the sentence.

The **square** is blue. 

The ________ is long. 

Ask me a ________. 

'q' sound /kw/

5. Unscramble me. Look at the picture. Unscramble the word to form its name.

k c u q i  quick

q l e a u 

u z e e e q s 

6. Read me. Read the sentence.

The red squid was quick

and quiet.

'q' sound /kw/

Story words: equal, question, queue, quick, quiet, square

7. **Read my story**. Look at the pictures. Read the story.

1

I want to ask my teacher a question. So, I quickly stand in the queue.

2

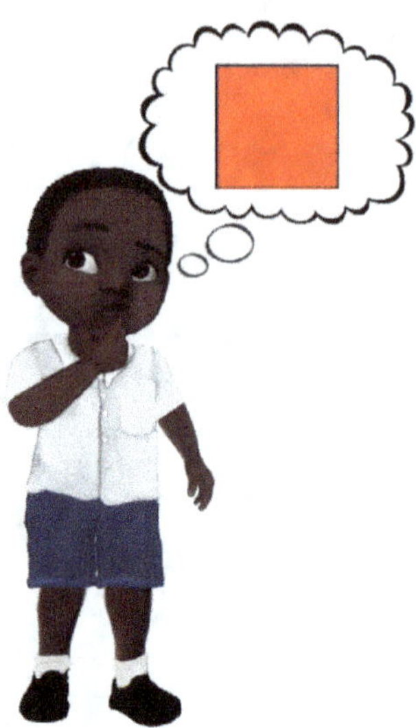

I want to know if squares have equal sides.

3

My teacher has to help many children.

4

I will be quiet and wait for my turn.

Say this word.
liquid
quill
square
Can you hear the /q/ sound?
Yes, I can!
Not sure.
No, I can't.

Theme: Sports

Sub-theme: Famous Jamaicans in sports

Term 2
/r/ sound: initial, medial and final positions

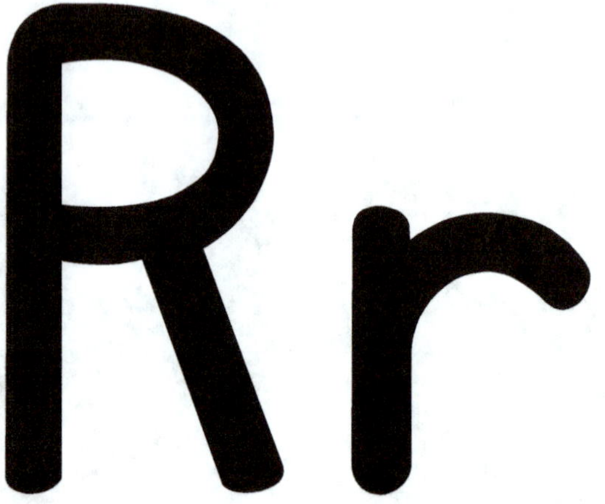
Rr

rope
perform
silver

rope

/r/ sound

1. Say my name. Point to each picture. Say its name.

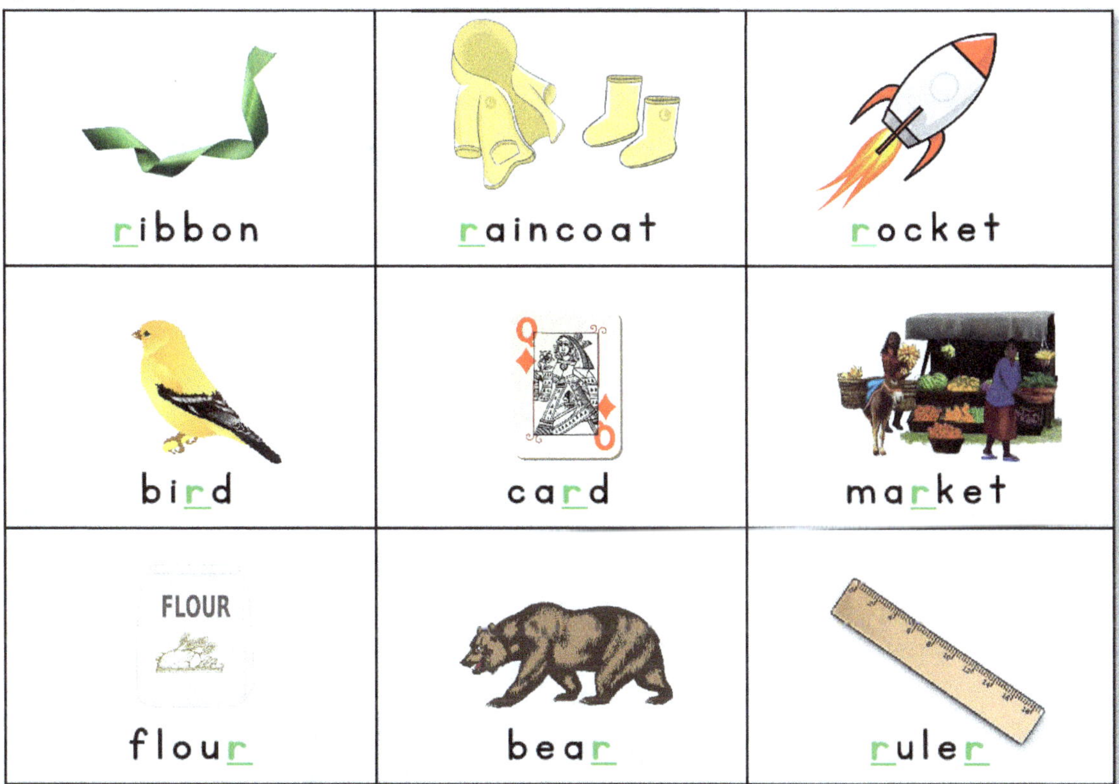

r i b b o n	r a i n c o a t	r o c k e t
b i r d	c a r d	m a r k e t
f l o u r	b e a r	r u l e r

2. Find my letters. Circle the letters then write the name.

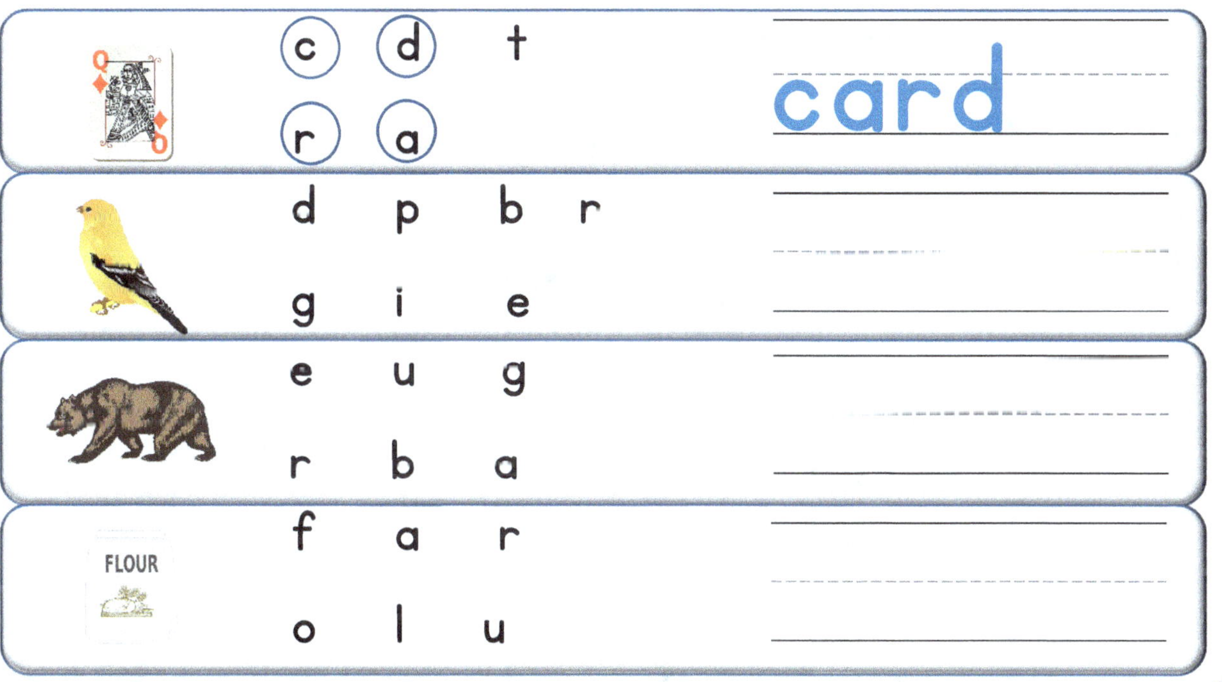

c d t r a			card
d p b r / g i e			
e u g / r b a			
f a r / o l u			

/r/ sound

3. Match me. Fill in the missing letter. Match the picture and its name.

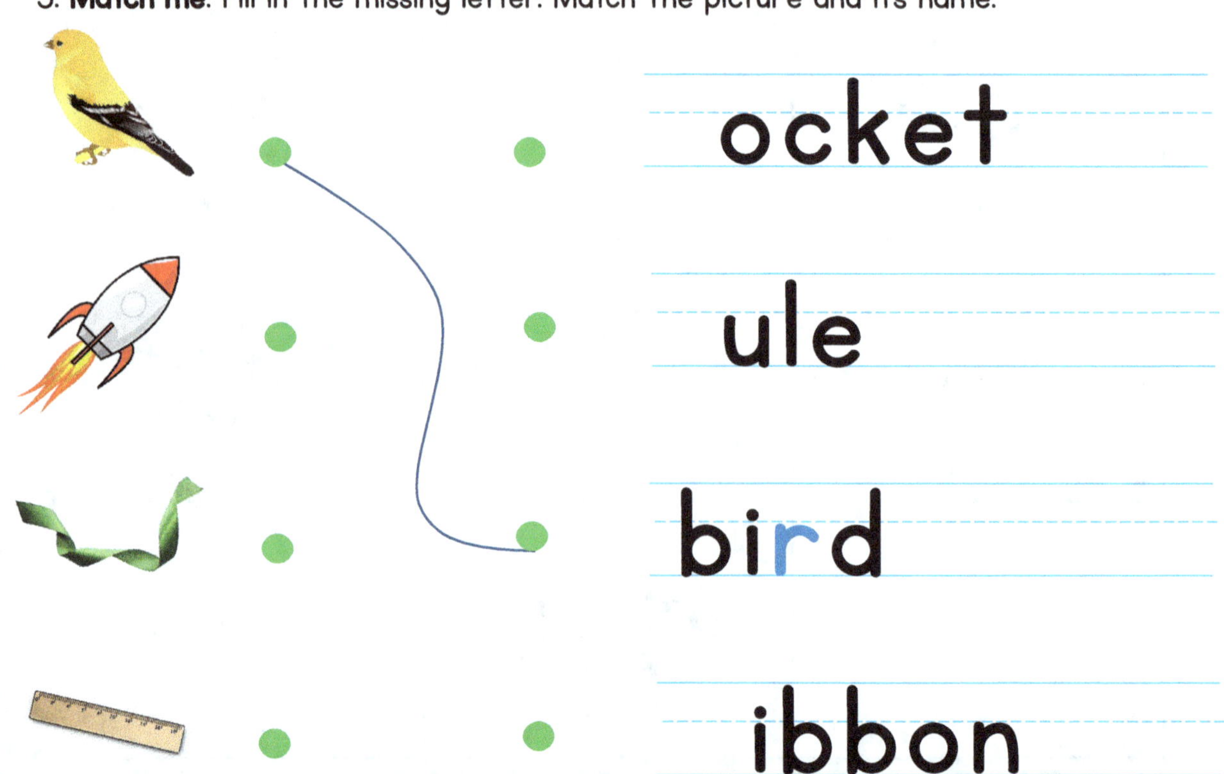

ocket

ule

bird

ibbon

4. Find my name. Say the word. Write its name.

Word bank

| market | flour | raincoat |

raincoat

FLOUR

/r/ sound

5. Check me. Look at the picture. Check the name. Write the name.

☐ **r**aincoat   ☐ **m**arket   ☑ **r**ibbon

ribbon

☐ bi**r**d   ☐ **r**ocket   ☐ flou**r**

☐ **r**ule**r**   ☐ ca**r**d   ☐ bea**r**

6. Read me. Read the sentence

Wear your **r**aincoat to

ma**r**ket and buy some flou**r**.

/r/ sound

Story words: ribbon, raincoat, bird, card, market, flour, bear

7. **Read my story**. Look at the pictures. Read the story.

Bird and Bear are planning a birthday party for butterfly.

"I'm going to the market to buy a raincoat. I want one with a ribbon."

"Please buy a birthday card and some more flour for the cake," says bird.

Oh, what a wonderful birthday party!

Say these words.
rope
perform
silver
Can you hear the /r/ sound?
Yes, I can!
Not sure.
No, I can't.

Term I

/s/ sound: initial, medial and final positions

S s

sandwich

ta**s**te

dre**ss**

dre**ss**

/s/ sound

1. Say my name. Point to each word. Say its name.

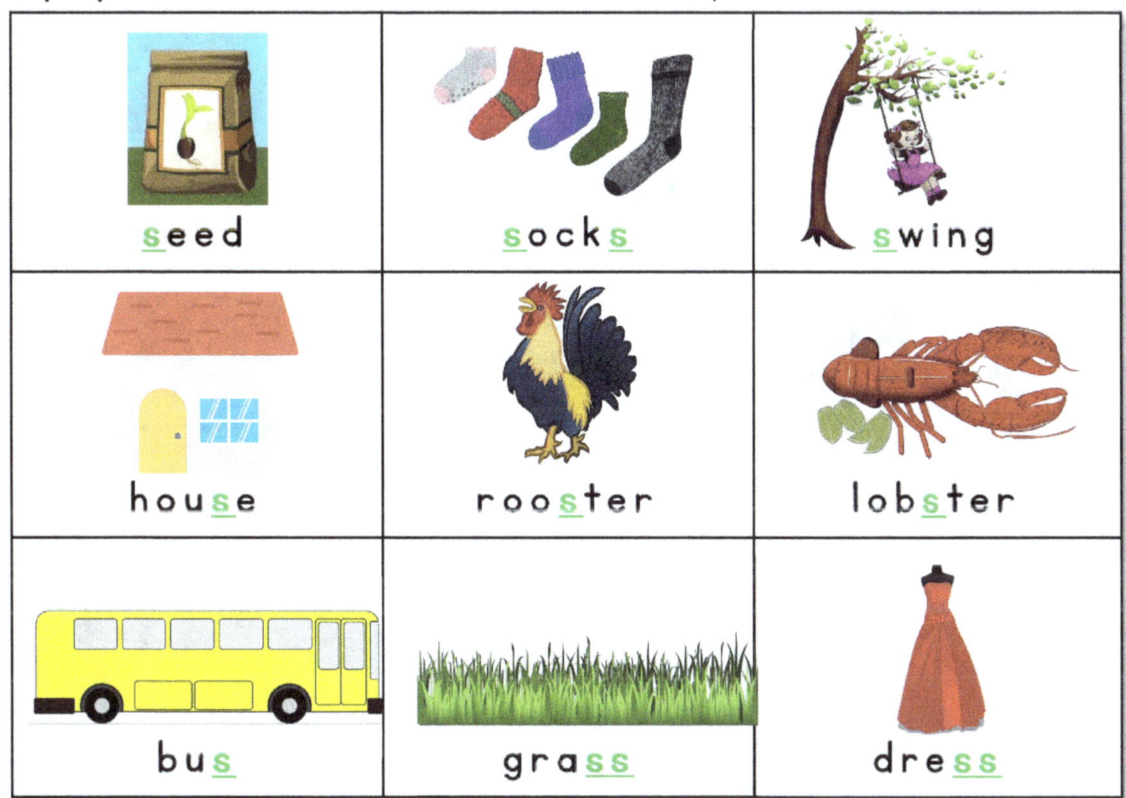

2. Find my name. Say the word. Write its name.

Word bank

socks   lobster   house

socks

____

____

____

/s/ sound

3. Match my parts. Circle the parts to make the name.

roo
lob s̲ter

gra
ss̲
dre

gra
ss̲
cla

mon
s̲ter
lob

4. Add my letter. Write the word. Circle the picture.

swing
swing

seed

bus

5. Unscramble me. Look at the picture. Unscramble the word to form its name.

s e s e d  seeds

s g s a r 

r s d s e 

6. Read me. Read the sentence.

Plant the gra<u>ss</u> <u>s</u>eed<u>s</u> next

to the hou<u>s</u>e.

/s/ sound

7. Read my story. Look at the pictures. Read the story.

It is spring. A man plants seeds near his hen house. A rooster walks by.

His daughter is sitting on the swing waiting for the bus.

She wears a bright yellow dress. Her shadow is on the grass.

Here comes the bus! She waves goodbye to her father.

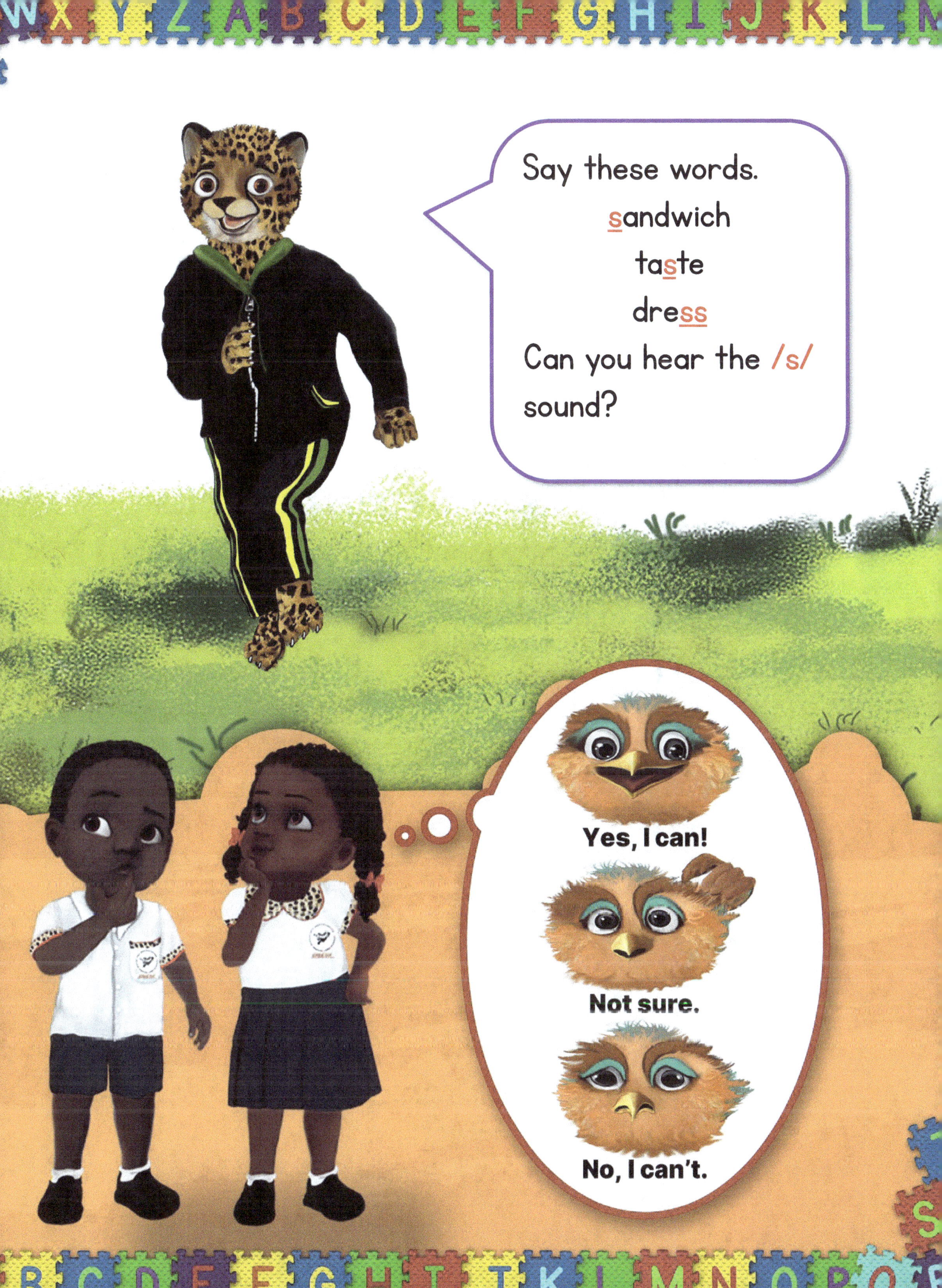
Say these words.
sandwich
taste
dress
Can you hear the /s/ sound?
Yes, I can!
Not sure.
No, I can't.

Sub-theme: Our people from Africa

Term I

/t/ sound: initial, medial and final positions

Tt

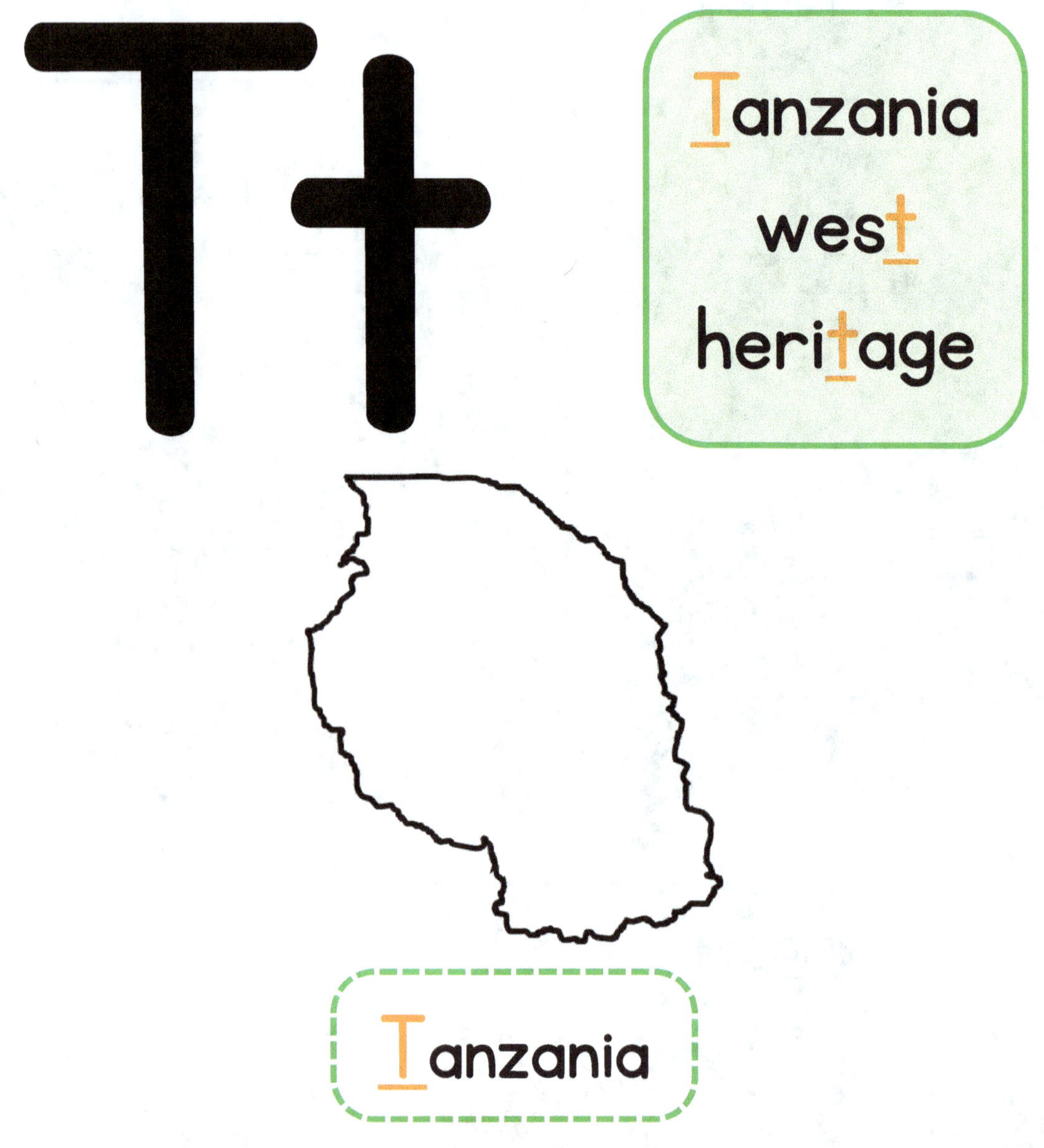

Tanzania

west

heritage

Tanzania

/t/ sound

1. Say my name. Point to each picture. Say its name.

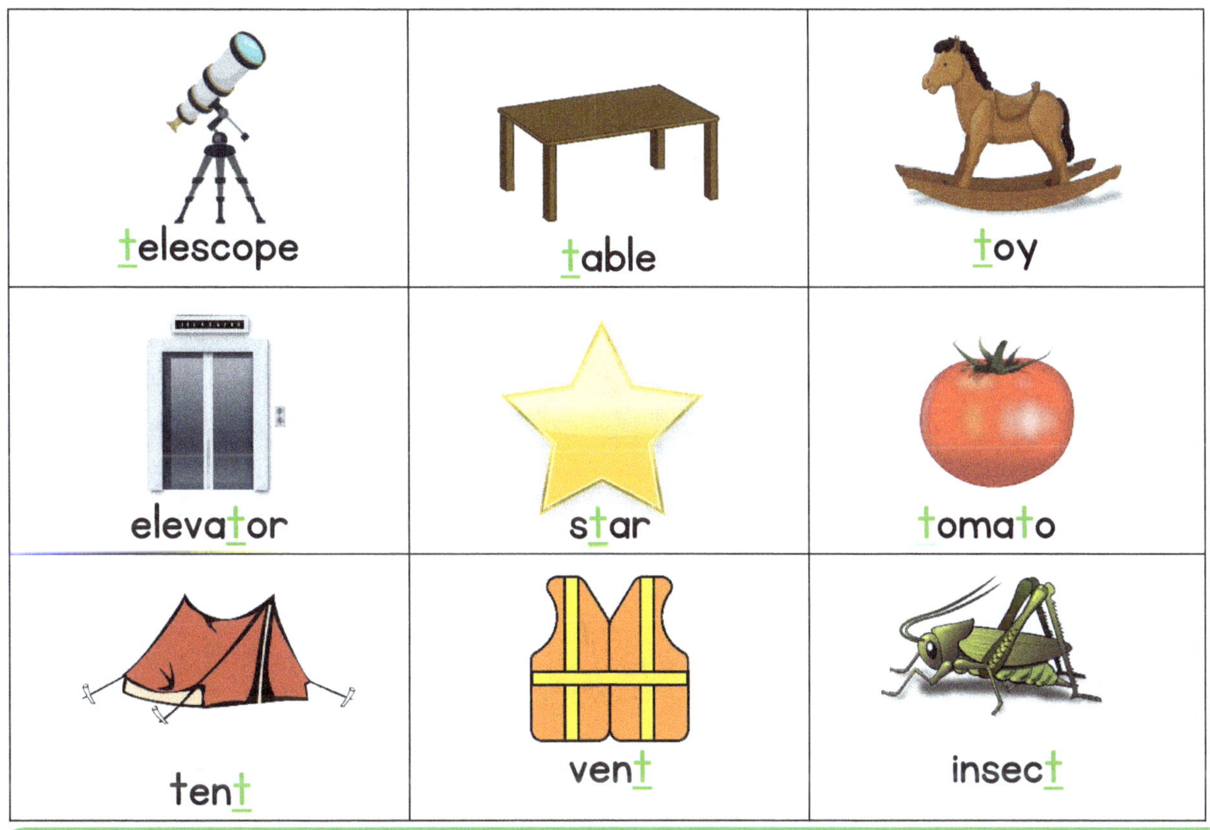

2. Add my letter. Write the word. Circle the picture.

/t/ sound

3. **Trace my name.** Circle the picture. Trace its name.

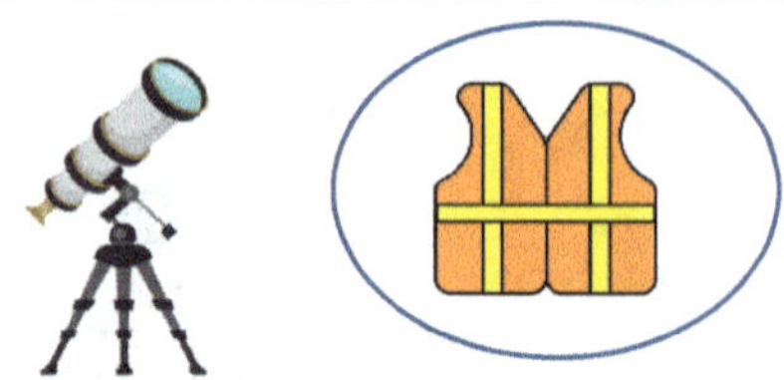

vest

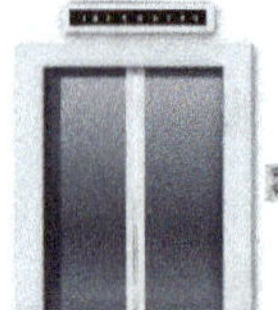

elevator

tent

4. **Write my name.** Write the name in the sentence.

Look at the table.

The __________ is red.

I like my __________.

5. **Check me**. Look at the picture. Check the name. Write the name.

☐ <u>t</u>oy   ☑ <u>t</u>elescope   ☐ ves<u>t</u>

telescope

☐ <u>t</u>omato   ☐ <u>t</u>able   ☐ <u>t</u>ent

☐ s<u>t</u>ar   ☐ insec<u>t</u>   ☐ <u>t</u>oy

6. **Read me**. Read the sentence.

Look at the s<u>t</u>ars through

the <u>t</u>elescope. 

/t/ sound

Story words: insect, star, telescope, tent, toy, vest, paint

7. **Read my story**. Look at the pictures. Read the story.

1

Sitting in his tent, the boy looks at the stars with his telescope.

2

An insect flies on his vest. He quickly brushes it off. It falls on his watch.

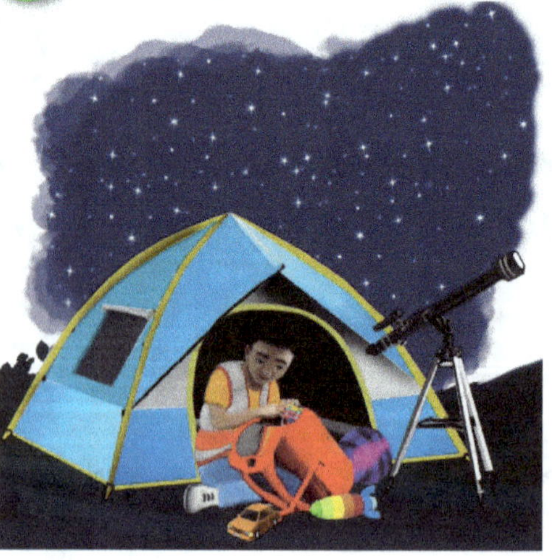

3

Oh my! It is time for bed. He packs his toys away.

4

Tomorrow, he will look for treasure with his telescope.

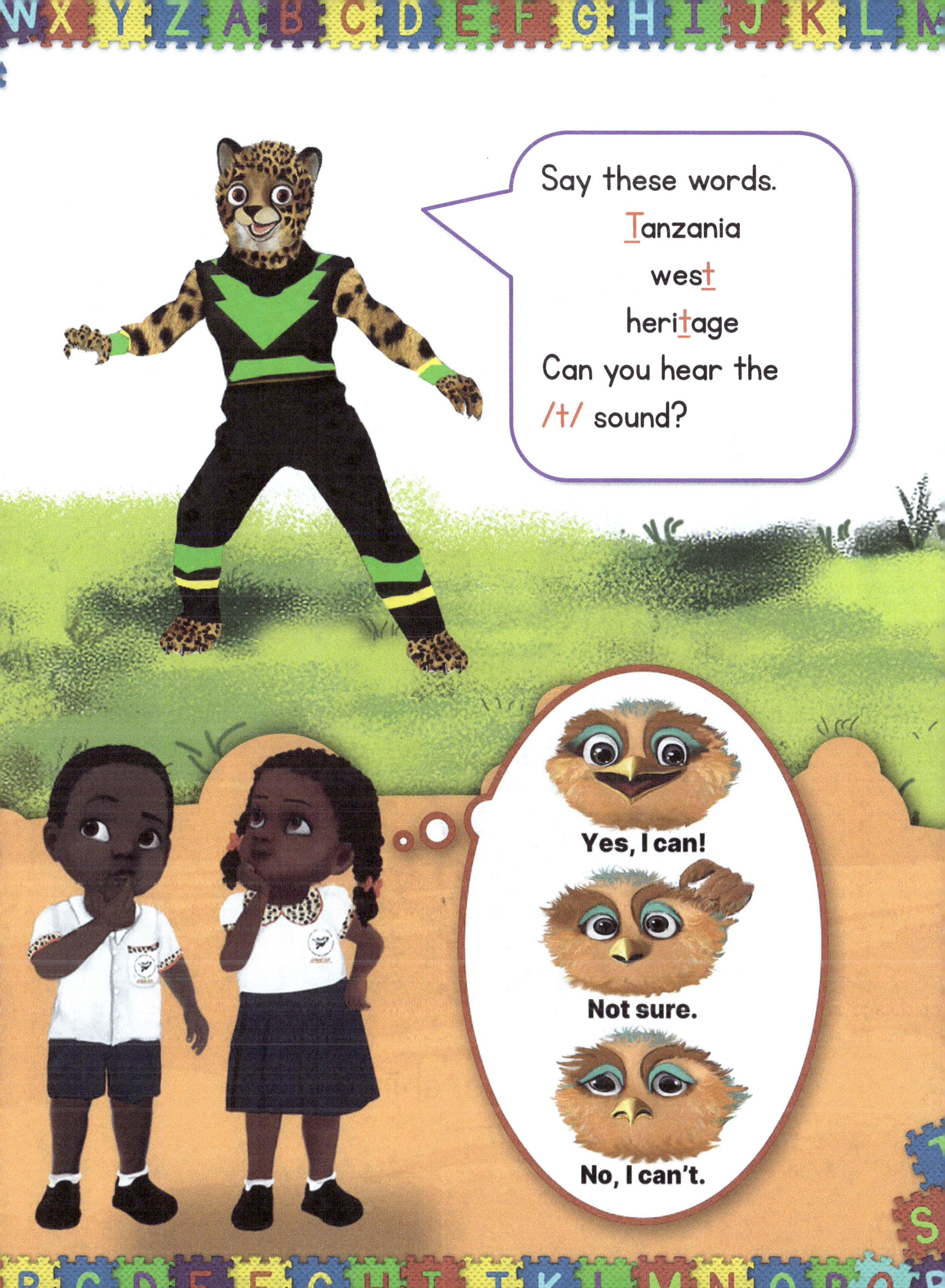
Say these words.
Tanzania
west
heritage
Can you hear the
/t/ sound?
Yes, I can!
Not sure.
No, I can't.

Term 3

short /u/ sound

Uu

undershirt

umbrella

underwear

undershirt

short /u/ sound

1. Say my name. Point to each picture. Say its name.

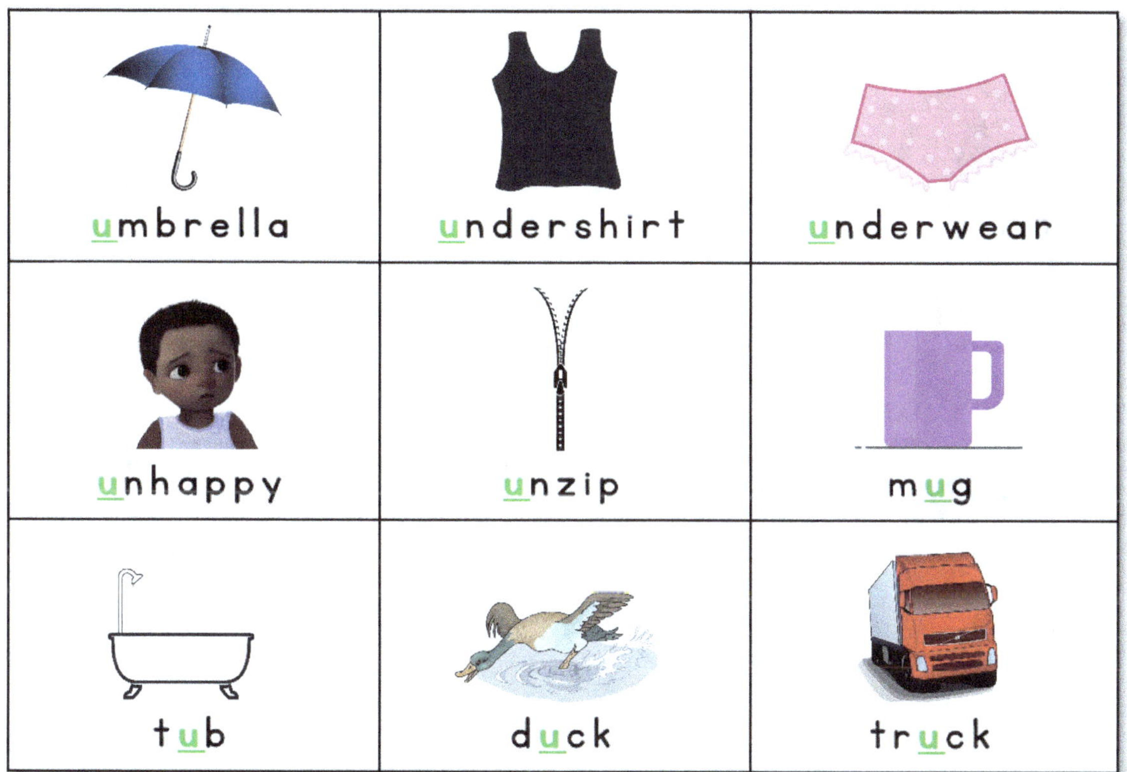

umbrella	**un**dershirt	**un**derwear
unhappy	**u**nzip	m**u**g
t**u**b	d**u**ck	tr**u**ck

2. Find my name. Say the word. Write its name.

Word bank

mug   truck   unzip

truck

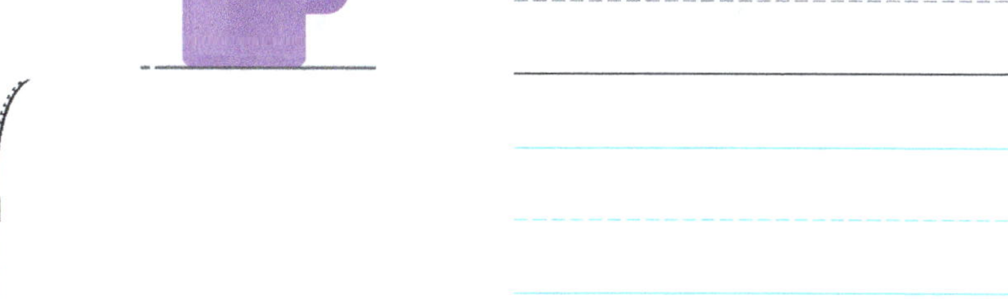

3. **Check me**. Look at the picture. Check the name. Write the name.

☐ **u**nhappy   ☑ **u**ndershirt   ☐ t**u**b

<u>undershirt</u>

☐ **u**mbrella   ☐ m**u**g   ☐ tr**u**ck

☐ tr**u**ck   ☐ **u**nderwear   ☐ d**u**ck

4. **Read me**. Read the sentence.

There is an **u**nhappy d**u**ck in the t**u**b!

5. Circle my name. Circle the name of the picture.

unhappy   d<u>u</u>ck   <u>u</u>mbrella   <u>u</u>nzip

tr<u>u</u>ck   <u>u</u>mbrella   t<u>u</u>b   <u>u</u>ndershirt

<u>u</u>nhappy   <u>u</u>nderwear   d<u>u</u>ck   <u>u</u>ndershirt

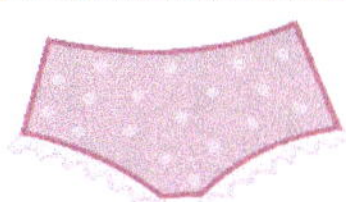
<u>u</u>nzip   <u>u</u>nderwear   m<u>u</u>g   t<u>u</u>b

6. Find my letters. Circle the letters then write the name.

g   c   m
t   u   a

mug

c   t   b   k
r   c   u

____

u   l   t
a   b   j

____

s   k   e
d   u   c

____

short /u/ sound

Story words: duck, tub, umbrella, undershirt, underwear

7. **Read my story**. Look at the pictures. Read the story.

1

It is raining.

2

Mark is getting dressed for school. He puts on his underwear and undershirt.

3

He is ready. He grabs his umbrella and goes outside.

4

He likes getting wet in the tub with his rubber duck, not in the rain.

Say these words.
duck
mug
underwear
Can you hear the /u/ sound?
Yes, I can!
Not sure.
No, I can't.

/v/ sound: initial and medial positions

Vv

valley

/v/ sound

1. Say my name. Point to each picture. Say its name.

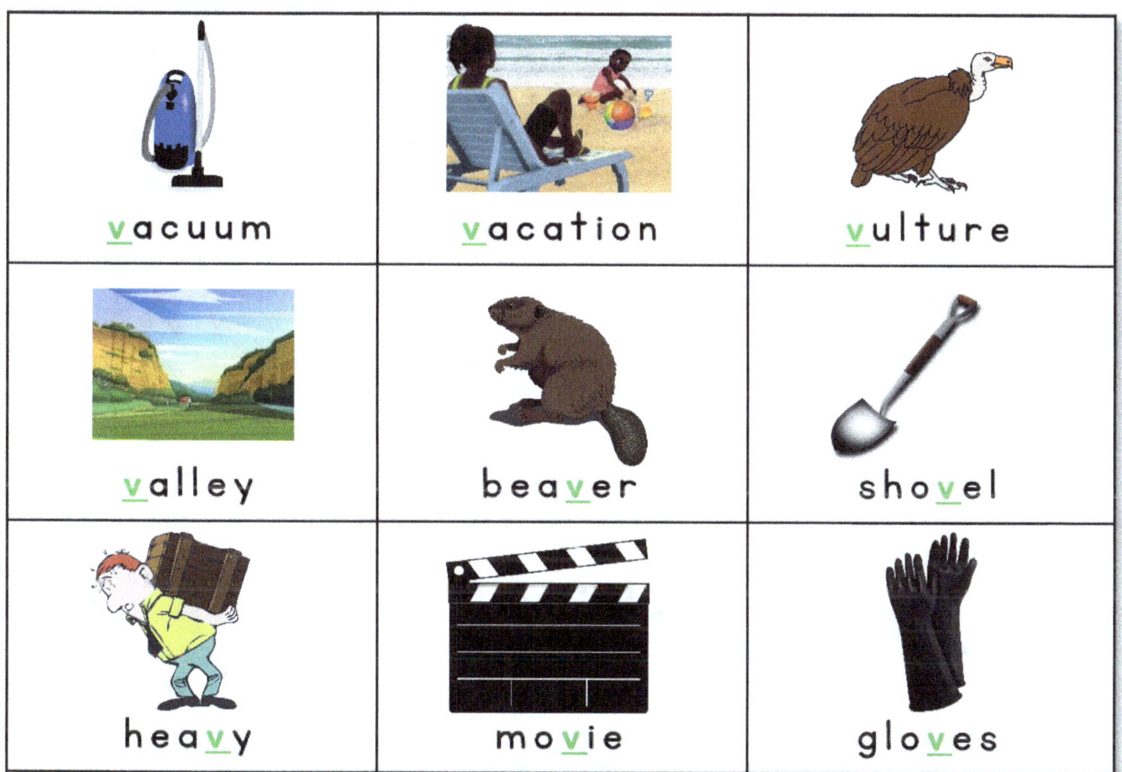

vacuum	**v**acation	**v**ulture
valley	bea**v**er	sho**v**el
hea**v**y	mo**v**ie	glo**v**es

2. Find my name. Say the word. Write its name.

Word bank

gloves   shovel   vacation

gloves

/v/ sound

3. **Add my letter**. Write the word. Circle the picture.

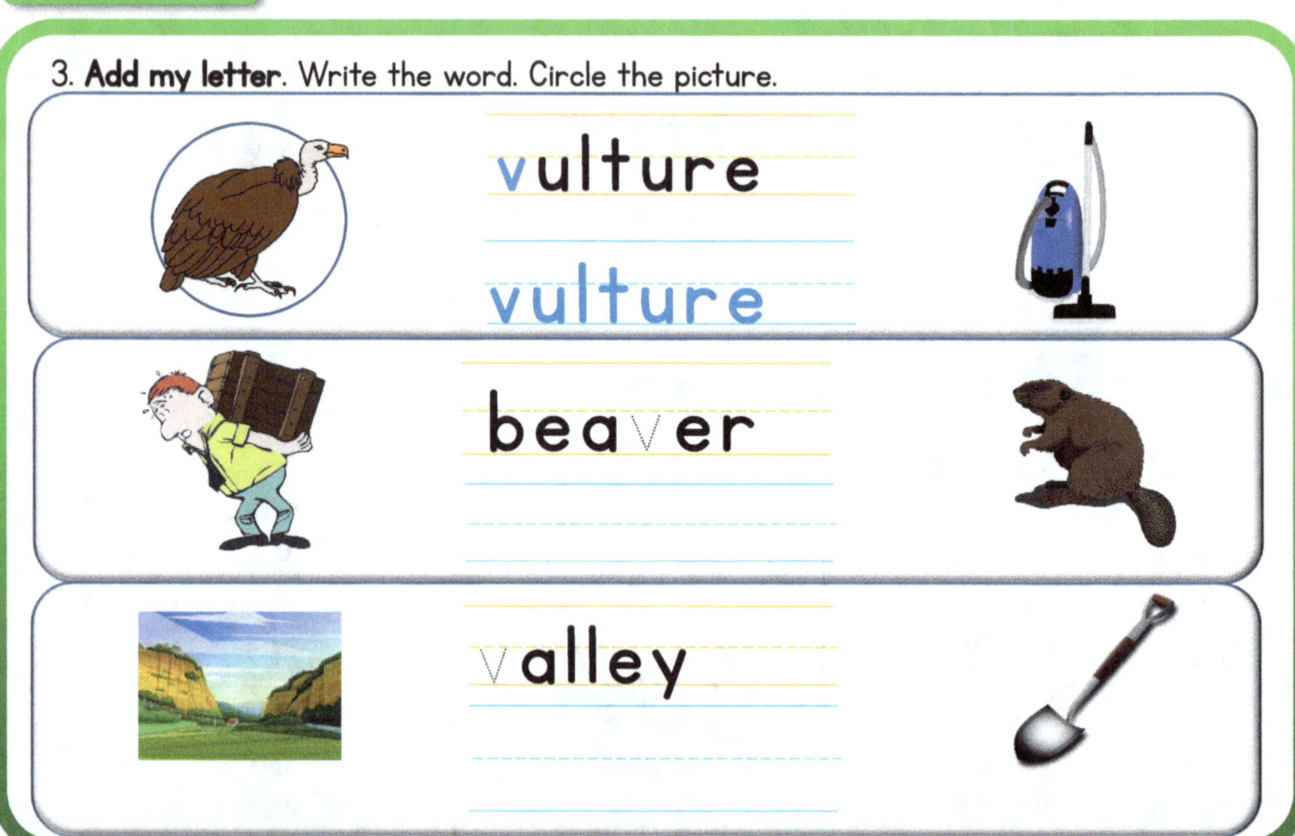

vulture

vulture

beaver

valley

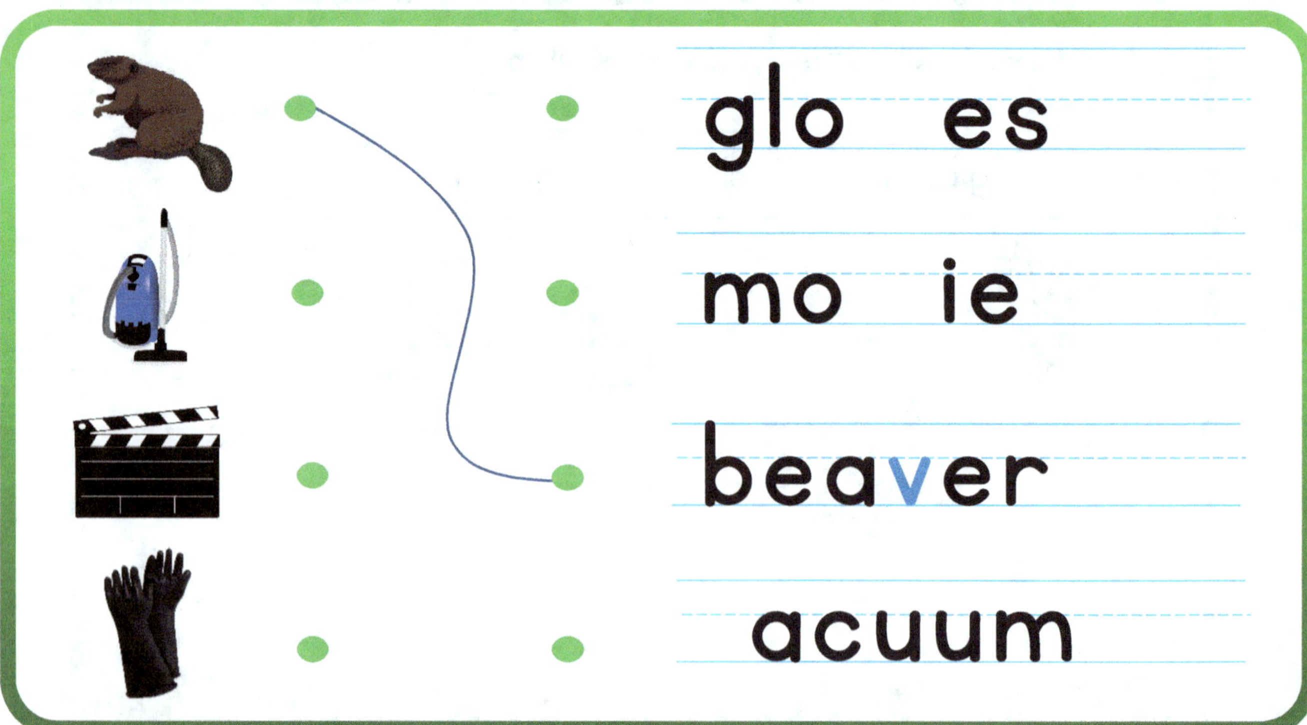

glo es

mo ie

beaver

acuum

5. Unscramble me. Look at the picture. Unscramble the word to form its name.

i v o e m 

c u m u v a 

v h y a e 

6. Read me. Read the sentence.

I saw a bea**v**er and a **v**ulture

in the **v**alley.

/v/ sound

Story words: gloves, heavy, movie, vacation, vacuum, vulture

7. **Read my story**. Look at the pictures. Read the story.

Vulture likes to clean with his new vacuum.

He puts on his gloves and moves the heavy furniture.

Now he can clean behind it.

Vulture is tired. "I want a vacation," he says. "Until then, I will watch a movie"

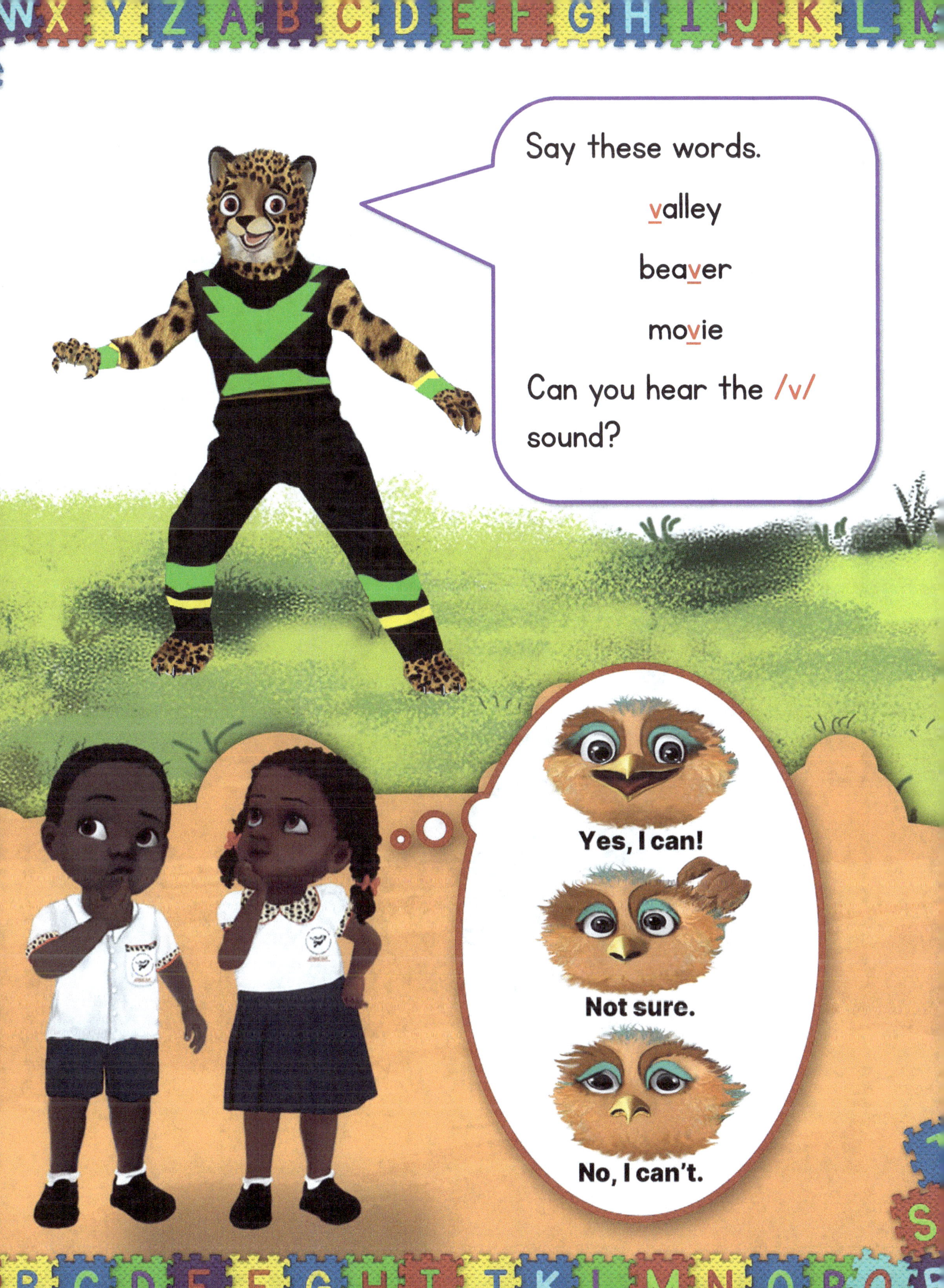

Say these words.
valley
beaver
movie
Can you hear the /v/ sound?
Yes, I can!
Not sure.
No, I can't.

Theme: The weather

Sub-theme: What is the weather like?

Term 3

/w/ sound: initial and medial position

Ww

weather
window
wow
willow
work

willow

/w/ sound

1. Say my name. Point to each picture. Say its name.

wagon	**w**heel	**w**heat
cro**w**n	**w**ig	**w**eb
water	**w**atch	to**w**el

2. Circle my name. Circle the name of the picture.

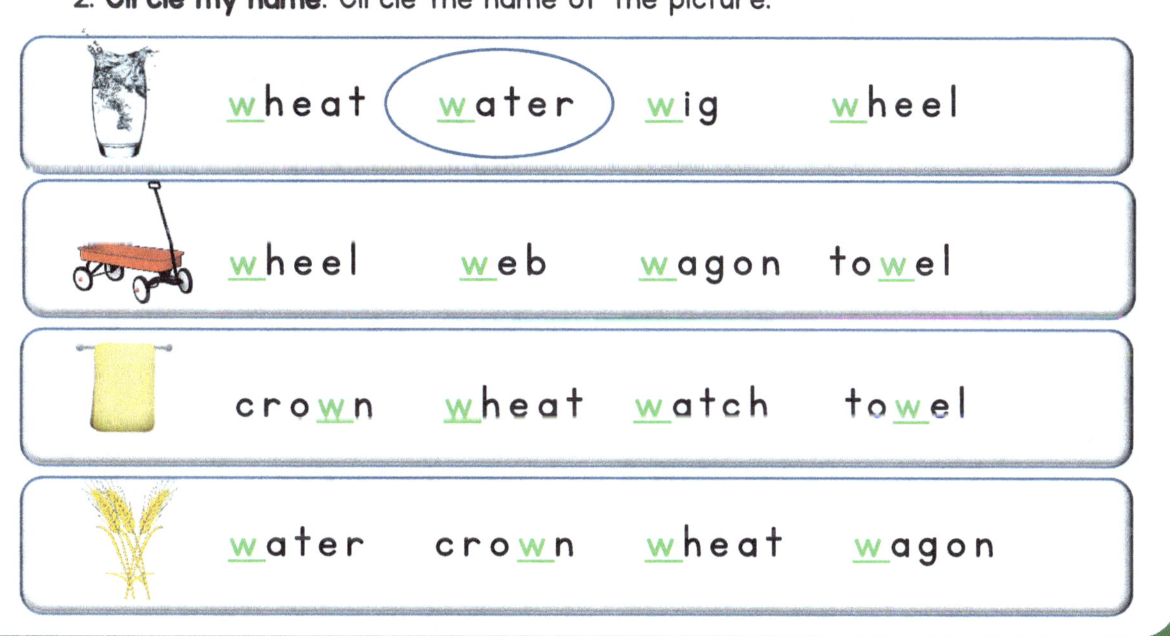

	wheat	**w**ater	**w**ig	**w**heel
	wheel	**w**eb	**w**agon	to**w**el
	cro**w**n	**w**heat	**w**atch	to**w**el
	water	cro**w**n	**w**heat	**w**agon

/w/ sound

3. **Add my letter**. Write the word. Circle the picture.

wheat

wheat

crown

towel

4. **Find my letters**. Circle the letters then write the name.

e	w	p
n	m	b

web

o	i	l
w	c	g

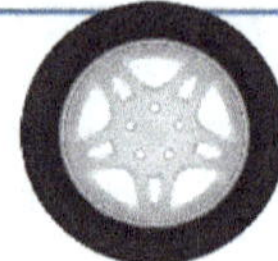

w	e	h
o	l	e

t	c	a
w	h	r

/w/ sound

5. Check me. Look at the picture. Check the name. Write the name.

☑ **w**ig   ☐ **w**heat   ☐ cro**w**n

wig

☐ to**w**el   ☐ **w**heel   ☐ **w**ig

☐ **w**eb   ☐ **w**atch   ☐ **w**agon

6. Read me. Read the sentence.

Watch the **w**heat and **w**ater in the pan.

/w/ sound

Story words: crown, wagon, water, wheat, wheels

7. Read my story. Look at the pictures. Read the story.

1

Wayne has a new wagon with shiny wheels.

2

He uses it to carry wheat and water for his animals.

3

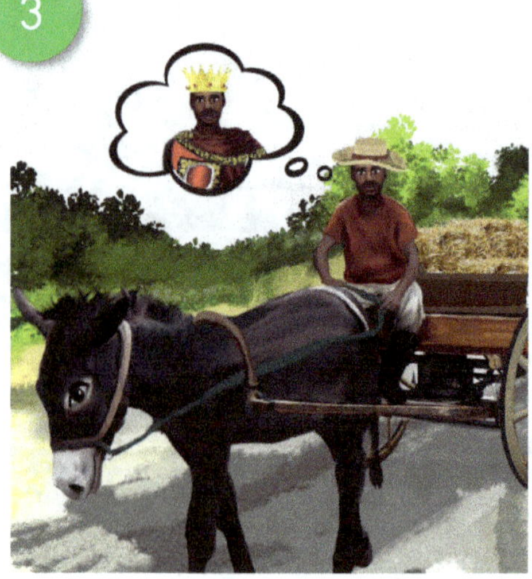

He loves riding his wagon. He feels like a king wearing a new crown.

4

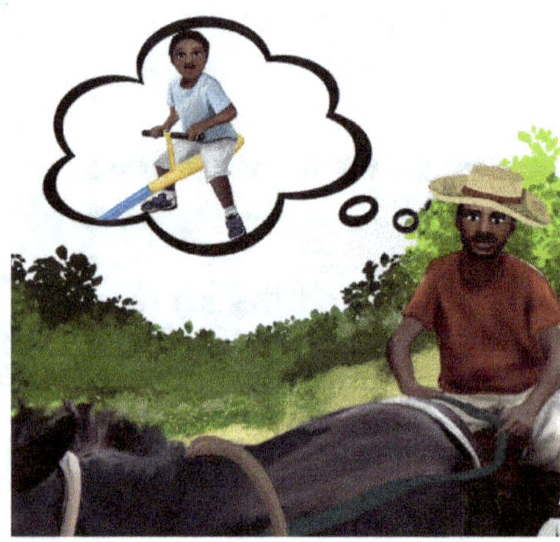

He feels like a child on a new toy.

Say these words.
window
bowl
crown
Can you hear the /w/ sound?

Yes, I can!

Not sure.

No, I can't.

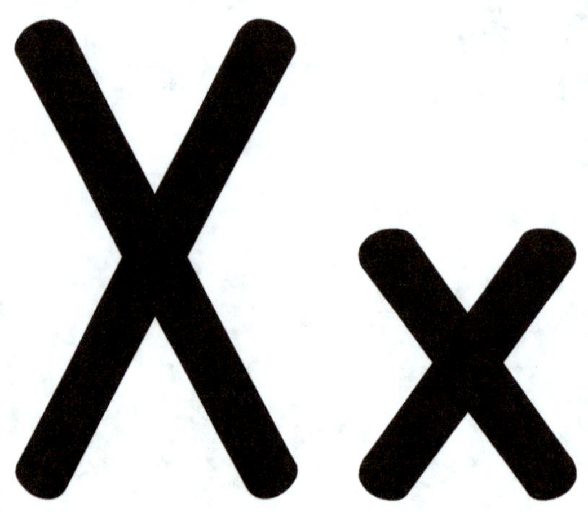

mi<u>x</u>er

'x' sound /ks/

1. Say my name. Point to each picture. Say its name.

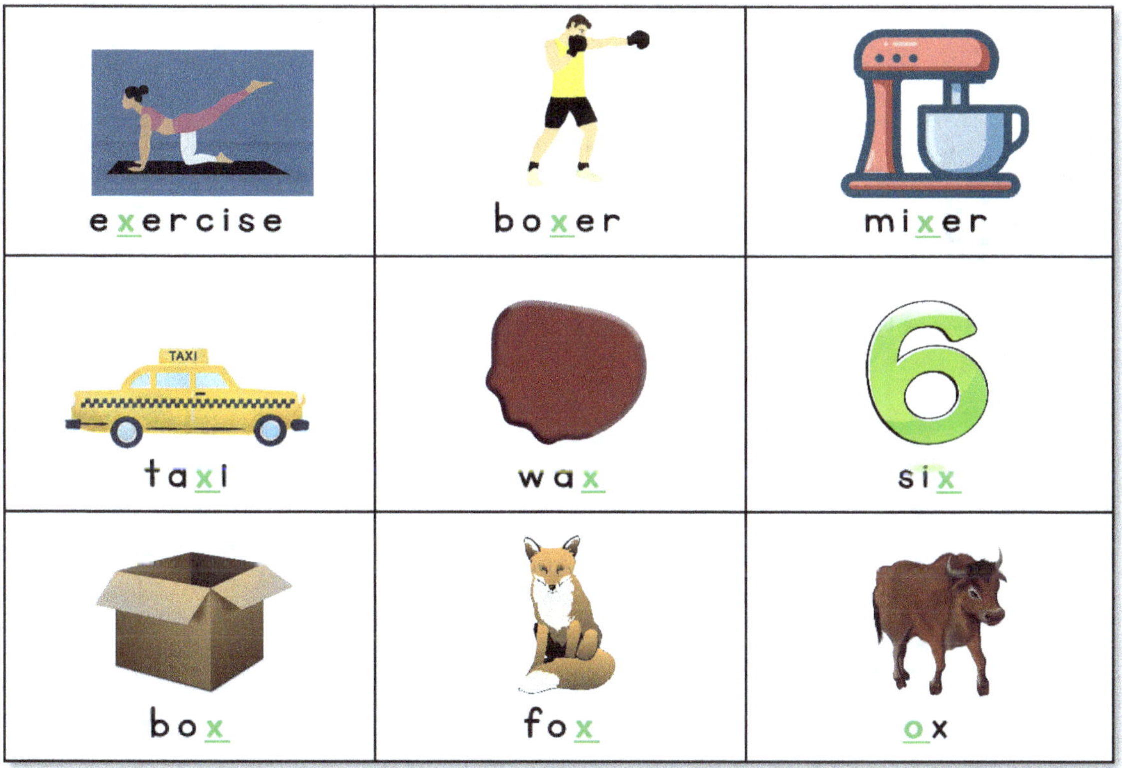

2. Match me. Fill in the missing letter. Match the picture and its name.

'x' sound /ks/

3. **Check me.** Look at the picture. Check the name. Write the name.

☐ ta<u>x</u>i   ☑ e<u>x</u>ercise   ☐ o<u>x</u>

exercise

☐ mi<u>x</u>er   ☐ wa<u>x</u>   ☐ si<u>x</u>

☐ bo<u>x</u>   ☐ bo<u>x</u>er   ☐ fo<u>x</u>

4. **Read me.** Read the sentence.

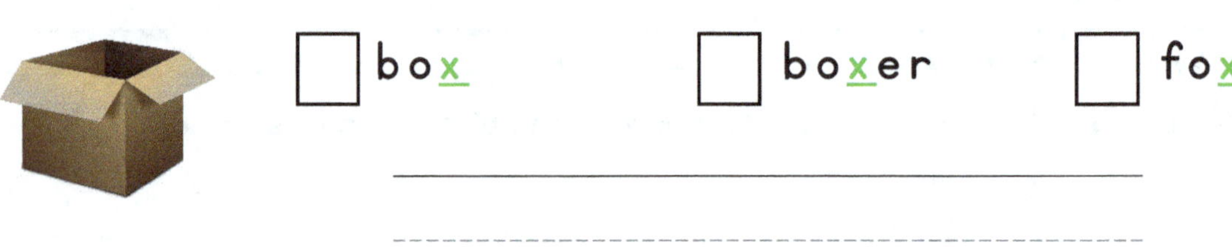

The bo<u>x</u>er took a ta<u>x</u>i to

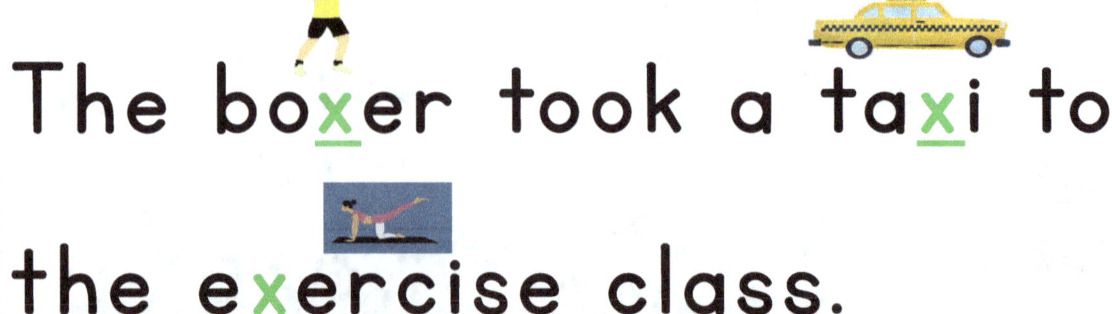

the e<u>x</u>ercise class.

'x' sound /ks/

5. Add my letter. Write the word. Circle the picture.

6

wax

wax

boxer

fox

6. Write my name. Write the name in the sentence.

Let's take a taxi. 

The __________ is big. 

Look in the __________. 

'x' sound /ks/

Story words: box, boxer, exercise, fox, ox, six

7. **Read my story**. Look at the pictures. Read the story.

Fox is a boxer.

He likes to box for exercise.

Each day, he boxes at six o'clock.

Sometimes, he boxes with an ox.

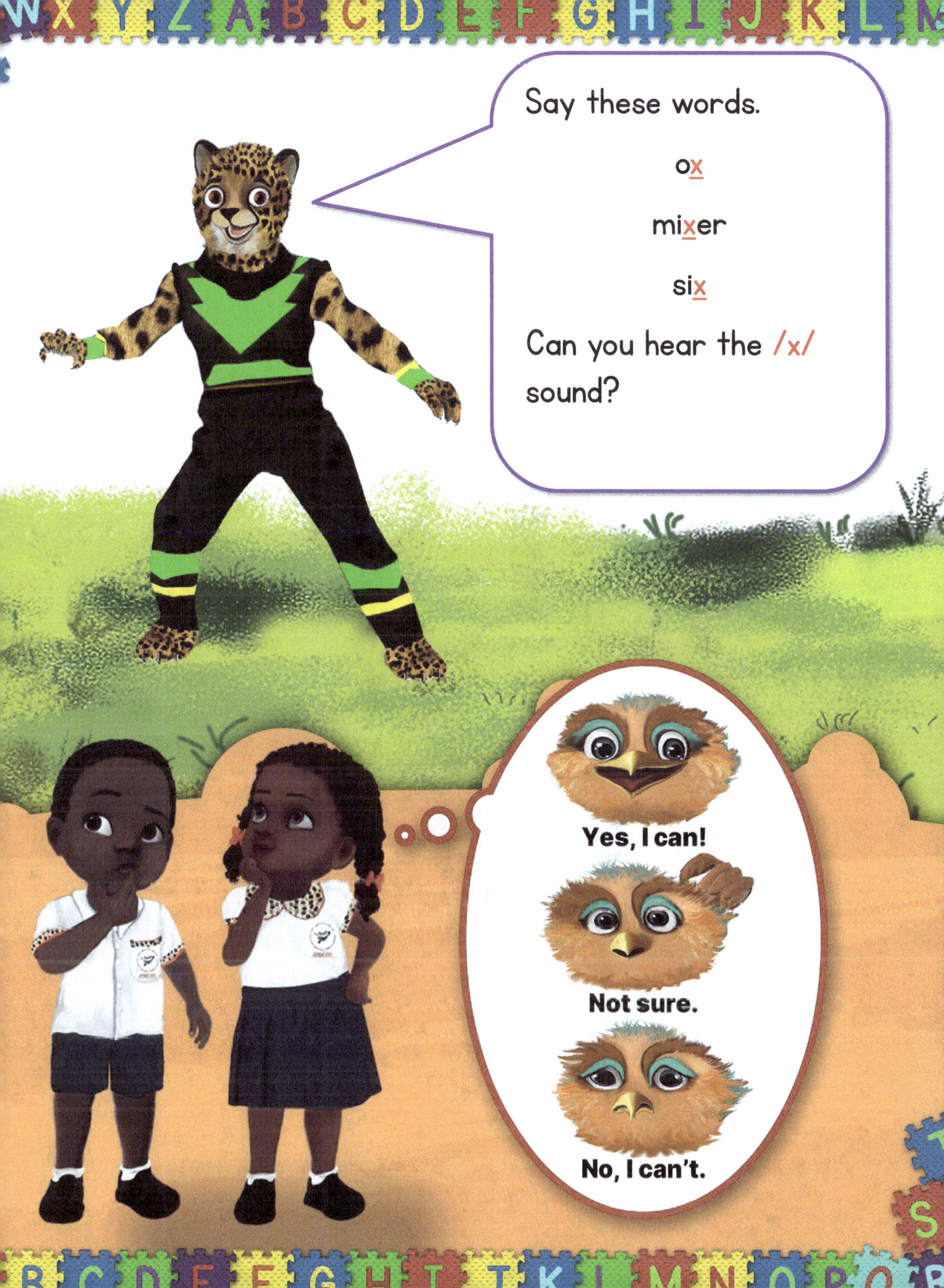

Say these words.
ox
mixer
six
Can you hear the /x/ sound?
Yes, I can!
Not sure.
No, I can't.

Yy

/y/ sound

1. Say my name. Point to each picture. Say its name.

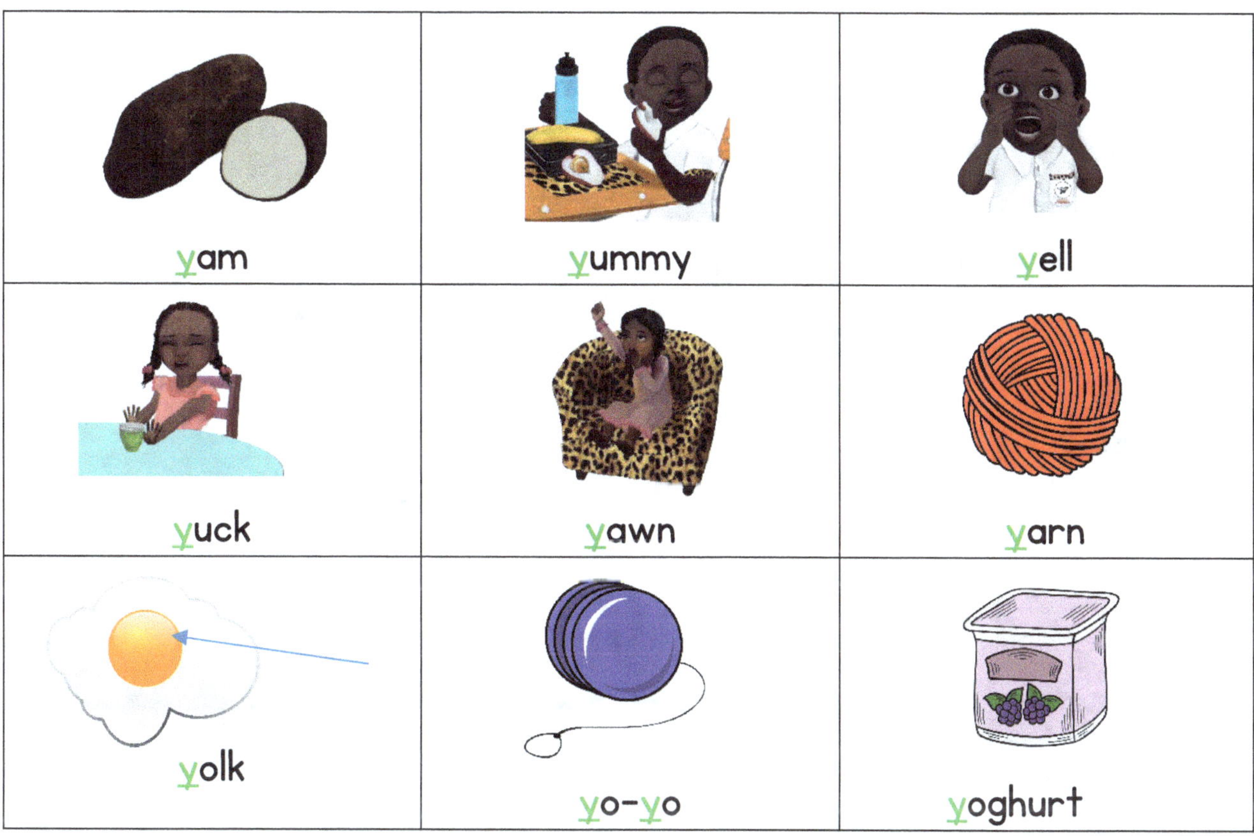

yam	yummy	yell
yuck	yawn	yarn
yolk	yo-yo	yoghurt

2. **Circle my name.** Circle the name of the picture.

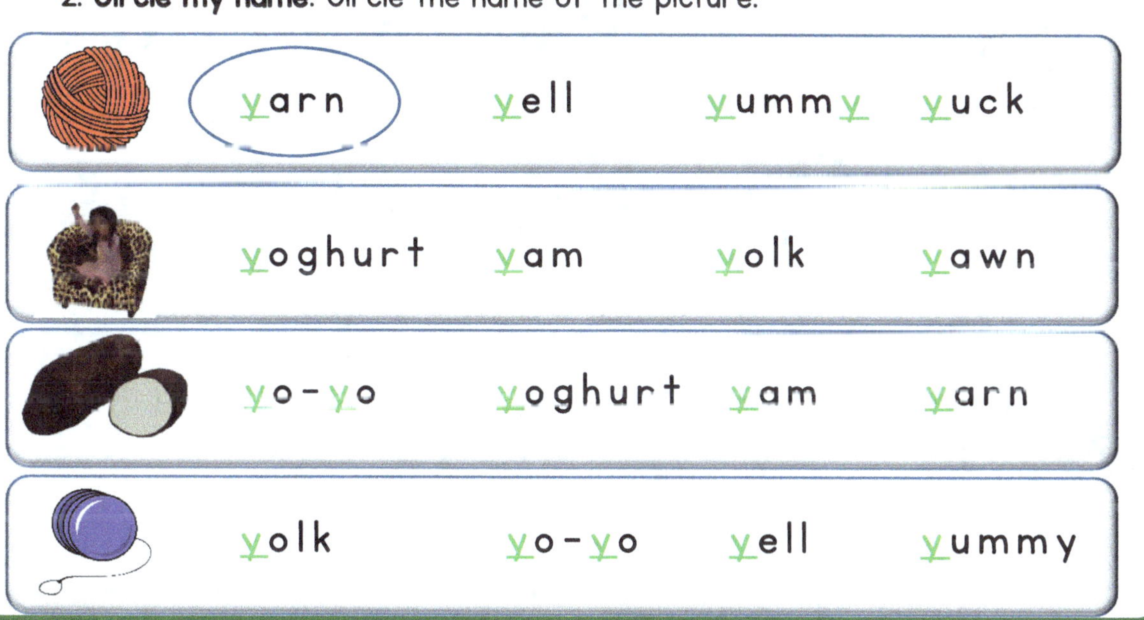

	(yarn)	yell	yummy	yuck
	yoghurt	yam	yolk	yawn
	yo-yo	yoghurt	yam	yarn
	yolk	yo-yo	yell	yummy

/y/ sound

3. Match me. Fill in the missing letter. Match the picture and its name.

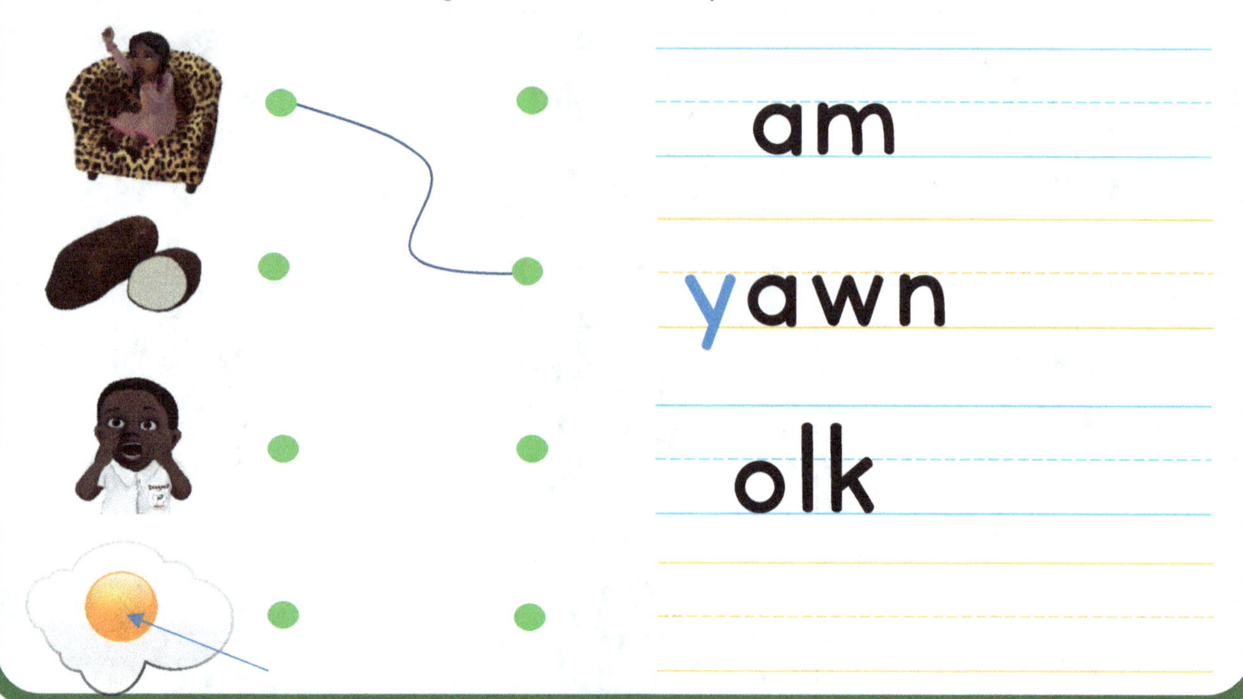

4. Trace my name. Circle the picture. Trace its name.

/y/ sound

5. **Unscramble me.** Look at the picture. Unscramble the word to form its name.

r a y n  yarn

o y y o 

c y k u 

6. **Read me.** Read the sentence.

Eat the yummy yolk and  yoghurt!

/y/ sound

Story words: yoghurt, yam, yells, yuck, yummy

7. **Read my story.** Look at the pictures. Read the story.

Yara does not like yams. She yells, "yuck!" when she sees them at dinner.

Her family thinks they are yummy.

What does Yara like? She likes yoghurt.

Mom smiles. "If you have yams for dinner, you can have yoghurt for dessert."

Say these words.
baby
candy
yam
Can you hear the /y/ sound?

Yes, I can!

Not sure.

No, I can't.

Term 3 — /z/ sound: initial, medial and final positions

Zz

buzz

/z/ sound

1. **Say my name.** Point to each picture. Say its name.

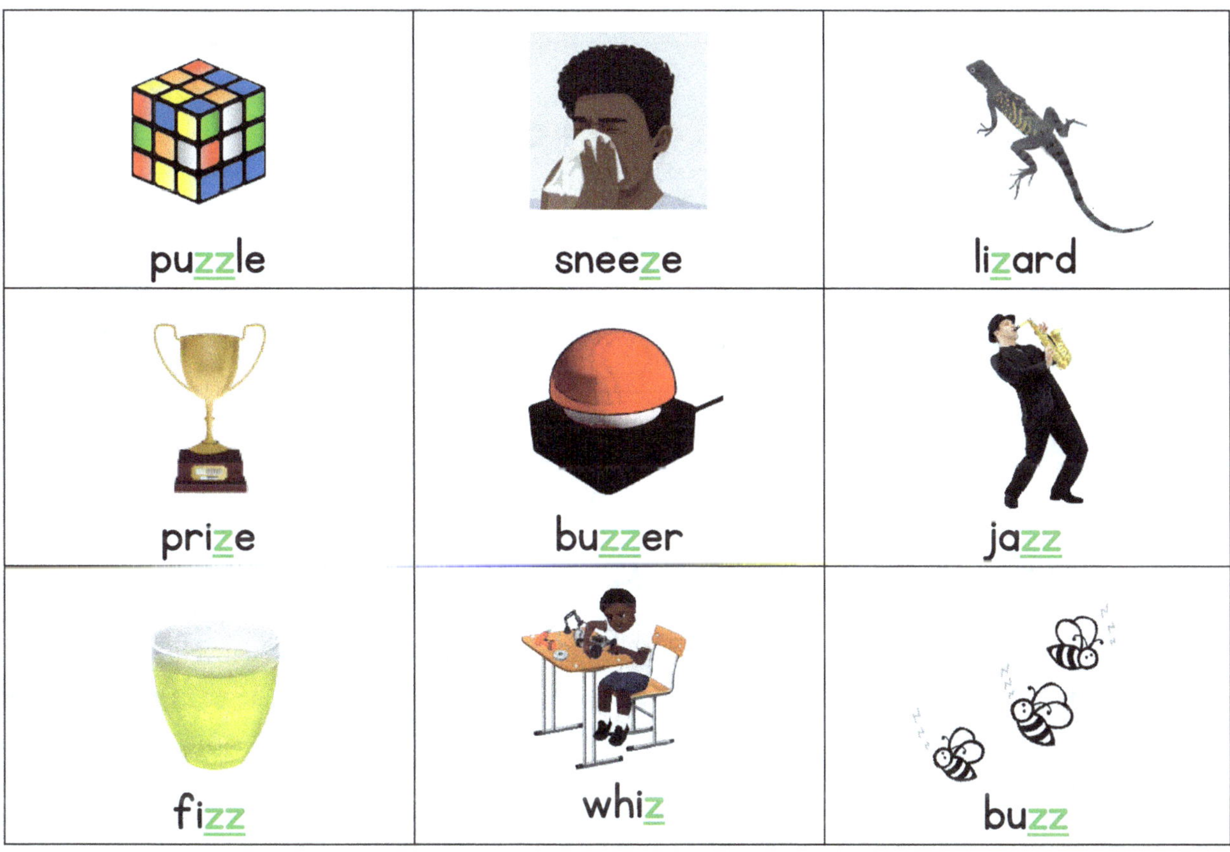

puzzle	sneeze	lizard
prize	buzzer	jazz
fizz	whiz	buzz

2. **Match me.** Fill in the missing letter. Match the picture and its name.

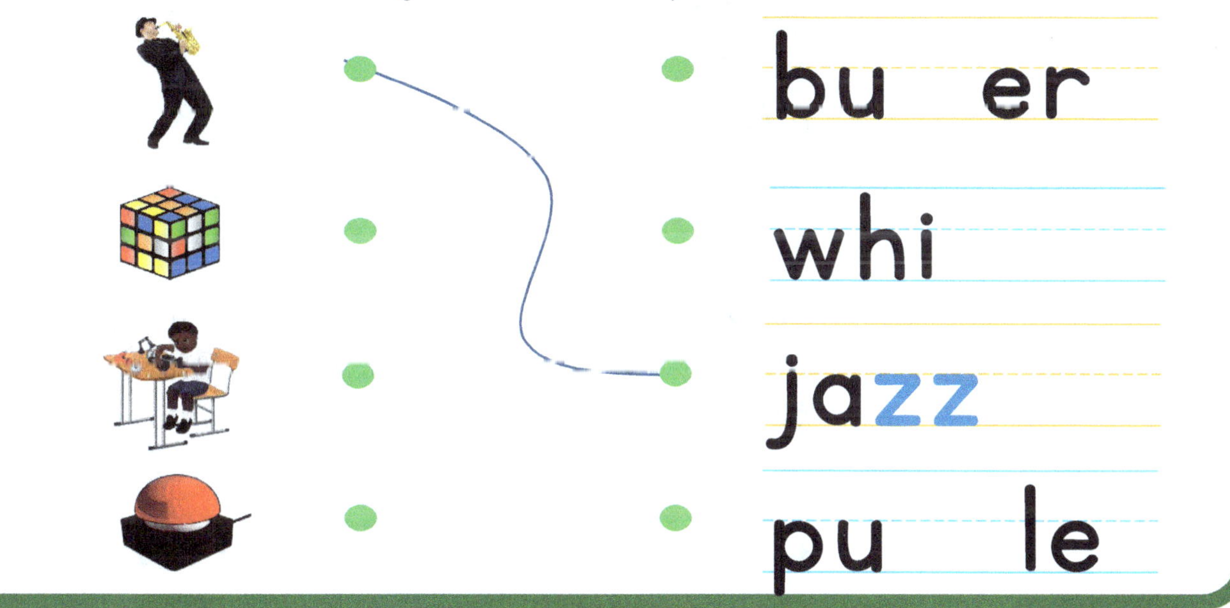

3. Write my name. Write the name in the sentence.

The <u>lizard</u> was fast. 

I'm going to __________. 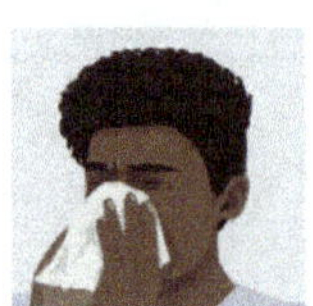

Hear the bees __________. 

4. Match my parts. Circle the parts to make the name.

snee / ze / free 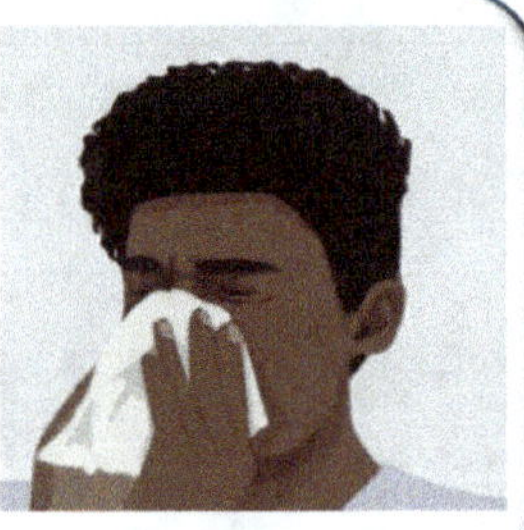

fi / zz / bu 

ja / zz / bu  

si / ze / pri 

5. **Circle then write my name**. Look at the picture. Circle its name. Write its name.

fizz

prize

fizz _______________

lizard

puzzle

____
____

jazz

waltz

____
____

6. **Read me**. Read the sentence.

Solve the puzzle and press the

buzzer to win a prize.

/z/ sound

Story words: buzz, fizz, lizard, puzzle, sneeze, whiz

7. Read my story. Look at the pictures. Read the story.

Have you ever heard a lizard sneeze?

What does it sound like?

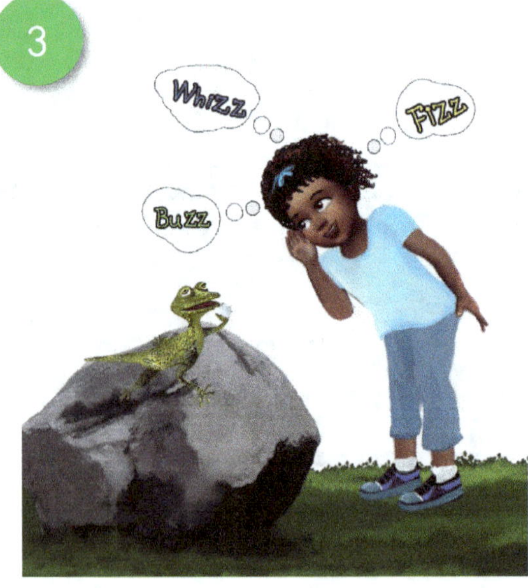

Does it sound like a buzz or a whiz?
Does it sound like a fizz?

It is a puzzle!

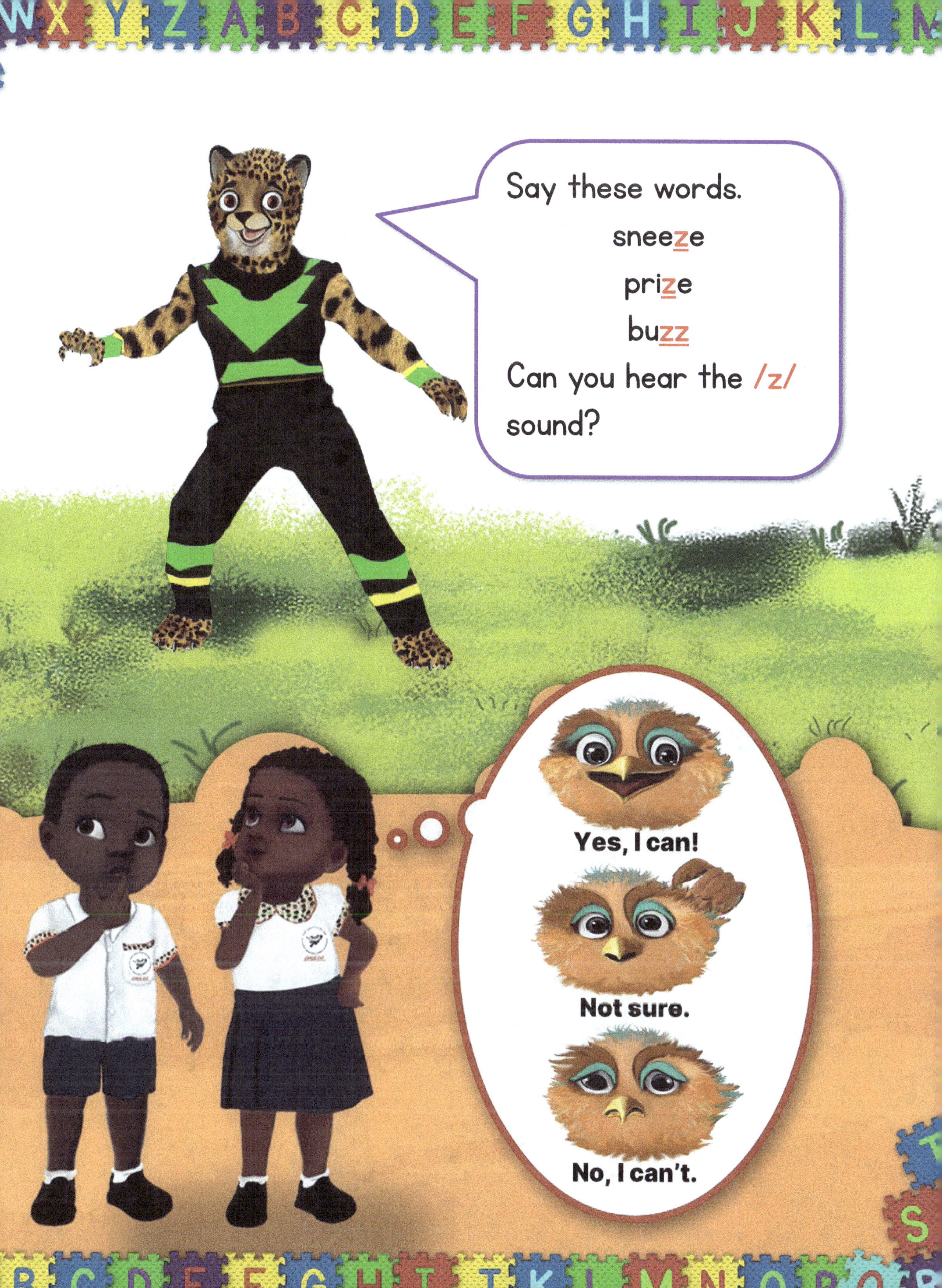
Say these words.
sneeze
prize
buzz
Can you hear the /z/ sound?
Yes, I can!
Not sure.
No, I can't.

Clusters and digraphs

Sub-theme: Our people from China

Term I

/ch/ sound: initial position.
Extended learning: /ch/ medial and final positions

ch

China
children
chest

China

/ch/ sound

1. Say my name. Point to each picture. Say its name.

cheese	child	chair
ketchup	kitchen	teacher
peach	lunch	bench

2. Circle my name. Circle the name of the picture.

chair   (teacher)   ketchup   lunch

child   peach   cheese   kitchen

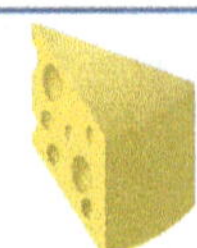
teacher   chair   cheese   bench

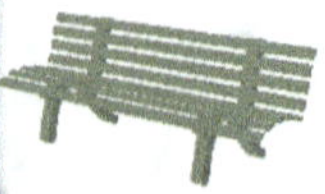
bench   ketchup   teacher   kitchen

/ch/ sound

3. **Trace my name.** Circle the picture. Trace its name.

lunch

child

chair

4. **Find my name.** Say the word. Write its name.

Word bank

bench   teacher   peach

teacher

5. Circle then write my name. Look at the picture. Circle its name. Write its name.

cheese

teacher

cheese

bench

lunch

peach

ketchup

6. Read me. Read the sentence.

The child sat on the chair

in the kitchen.

/ch/ sound

7. **Read my story**. Look at the pictures. Read the story.

Let's make lunch in the kitchen.

Here, my child, you can stand on a chair.

Do we use cheese, ketchup and peach?

Will you share it with your teacher?

Say these words.
China
teacher
lunch
Can you hear the /ch/ sound?
Yes, I can!
Not sure.
No, I can't.

Term 2 — /cl/ sound: initial position

clock

/cl/ sound

1. Say my name. Point to each picture. Say its name.

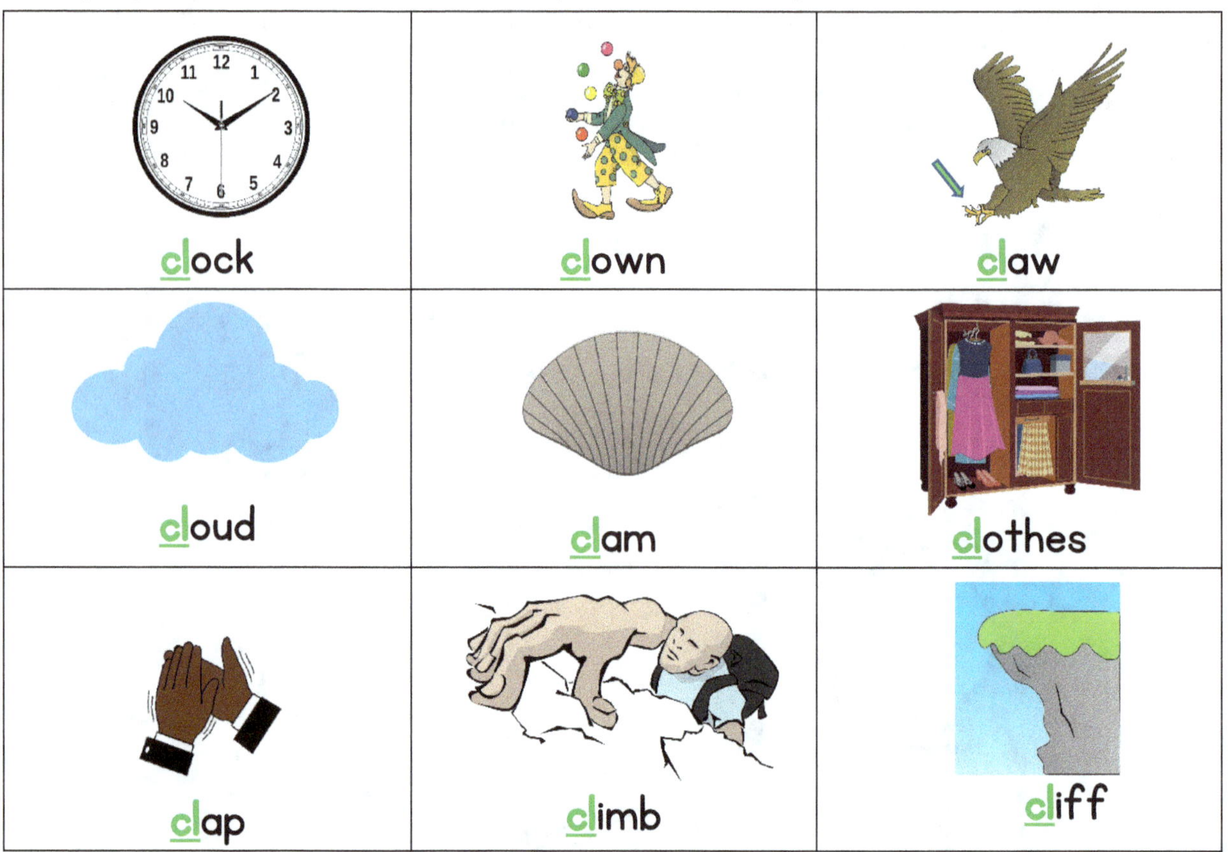

clock	clown	claw
cloud	clam	clothes
clap	climb	cliff

2. Add my letters. Write the word. Circle the picture.

clothes
clothes

clown

cloud

/cl/ sound

3. Circle my name. Circle the name of the picture.

(c l o c k)   c l a p   c l o t h e s   c l a w

c l o u d   c l i m b   c l o w n   c l a m

c i r c l e   c l a w   c l o c k   c l a p

c l o w n   c l i m b   c i r c l e   c l o t h e s

4. Write my name. Write the name in the sentence.

The   _cliff_   is tall.
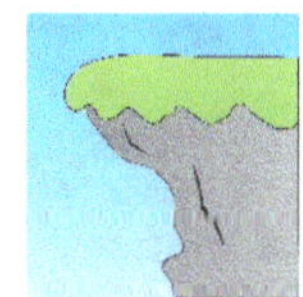

She has nice __________.

I hear a __________.

/cl/ sound

5. Unscramble me. Look at the picture. Unscramble the word to form its name.

k c o l c  clock

a l m c 

l w c a 

6. Read me. Read the sentence.

The **cl**own has a **cl**am on his

clothes.

/cl/ sound

Story words: claws, clock, clown, clap

7. Read my story. Look at the pictures. Read the story.

What time does the clock say? We will be at the circus soon.

At the circus, a clown, in funny clothes rides a tricycle in a circle.

People clap as a man lifts an acrobat.

Look at the tiger with big claws jumping through a fiery hoop.

Say these words.
clap
muscle
club

Can you hear the /cl/ sound?
Yes, I can!
Not sure.
No, I can't.

Sub-theme: We love to play

Term 2

/pl/ sound: initial position

/pl/ sound

1. Say my name. Point to each picture. Say its name.

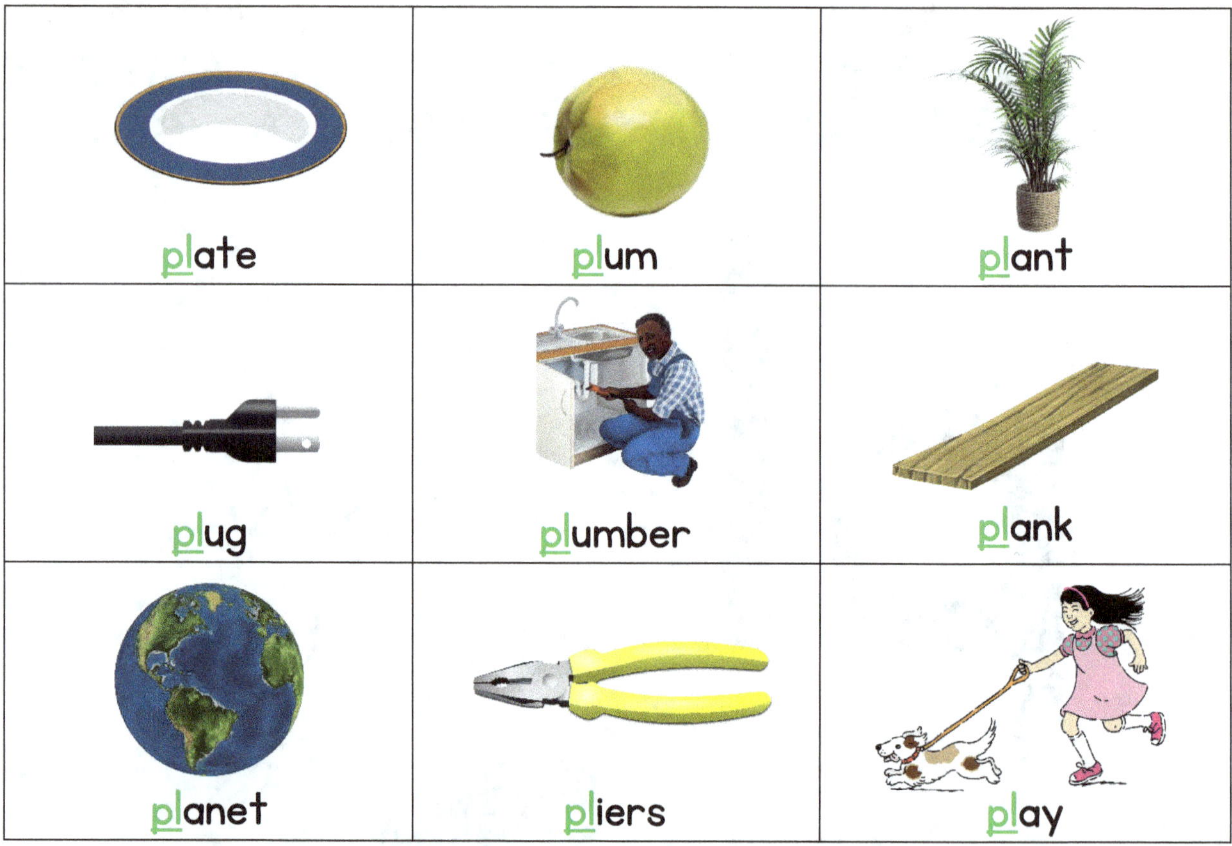

plate	plum	plant
plug	plumber	plank
planet	pliers	play

2. Find my letters. Circle the letters then write the name.

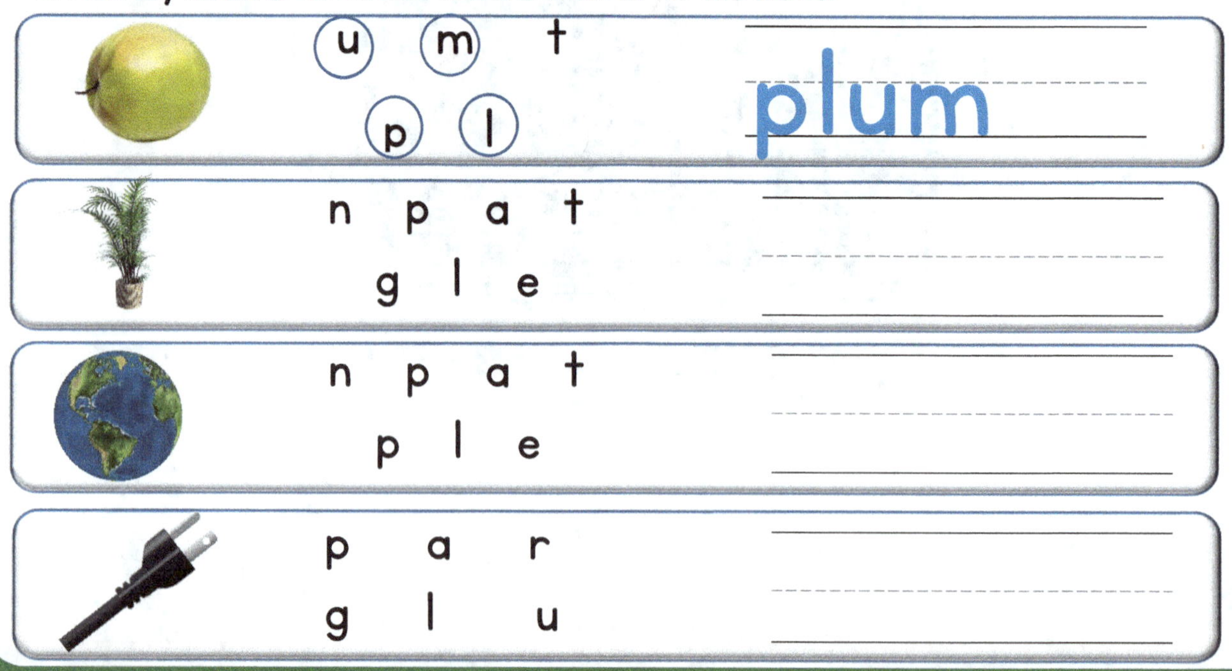

u m t p l		plum
n p a t g l e		
n p a t p l e		
p a r g l u		

/pl/ sound

3. Match me. Fill in the missing letter. Match the picture and its name.

umber

planet

pliers

ug

4. Find my name. Say the word. Write its name.

Word bank

plank   plate   play

play

5. **Check me**. Look at the picture. Check the name. Write the name.

☑ ☐ ☐

plumber

☐ **p**l**a**y   ☐ **p**l**a**nt   ☐ **p**l**i**ers

☐ **p**l**a**te   ☐ **p**l**a**net   ☐ **p**l**u**g

4. **Read me**. Read the sentence.

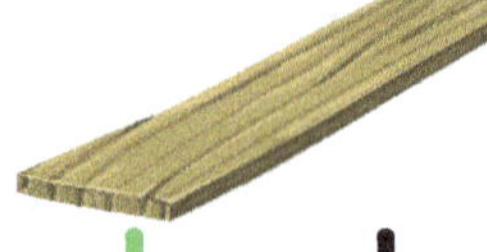

The **pl**umber puts the **pl**iers on the **pl**ank.

/pl/ sound

Story words: apple, people, plant, plate, plum, purple

7. **Read my story**. Look at the pictures. Read the story.

1

Sam has a purple plum and a red apple on his plate.

2

I will plant many seeds.

3

They will grow into trees.

4

I will plant the seeds so many people on the planet can get fruits.

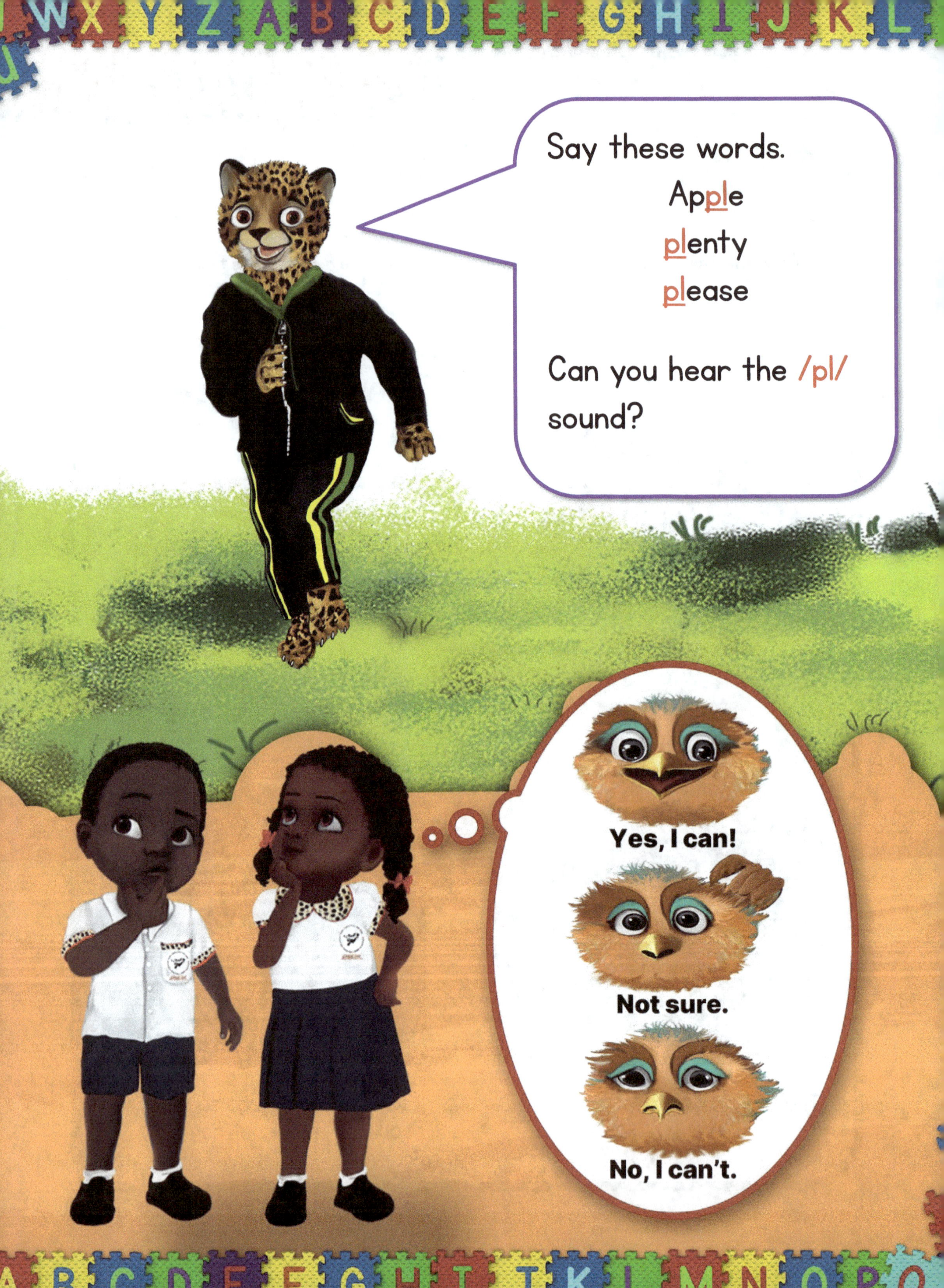

Say these words.
Apple
plenty
please

Can you hear the /pl/ sound?
Yes, I can!
Not sure.
No, I can't.

Term 2

/sh/ sound: initial position
Extended learning: medial and final positions

sh

sheltered
ship

ship

/sh/ sound

1. Say my name. Point to each picture. Say its name.

shell	**sheep**	**ship**
cushion	**mushroom**	**fishbowl**
fish	**bush**	**jellyfish**

2. Find my name. Say the word. Write its name.

Word bank

mushroom	fishbowl	jellyfish

mushroom

/sh/ sound

3. Match my parts. Circle the parts to make the name.

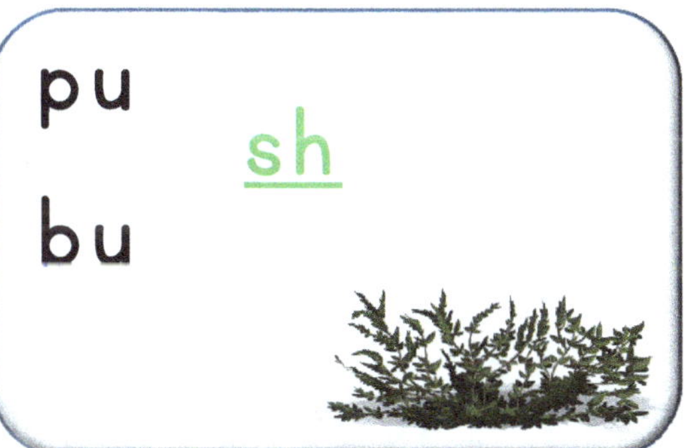

4. Add my letters. Write the word. Circle the picture.

bush
bush

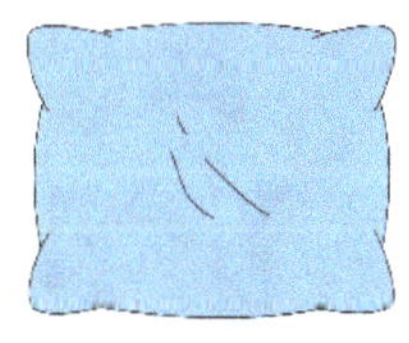
cushion

shell

CHEETAH® EARLY CHILDHOOD PHONICS

---

5. Unscramble me. Look at the picture. Unscramble the word to form its name.

h s e p e      **sheep**

i h s f   

s i p h   

---

6. Read me. Read the sentence.

   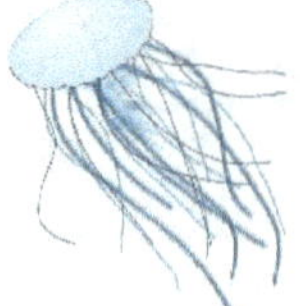

The fi<u>sh</u> and the jellyfi<u>sh</u> are

in the fi<u>sh</u>bowl.

/sh/ sound

Story words: bush, fish, fishbowl, jellyfish, sheep, shell, ship, shore

7. **Read my story**. Look at the pictures. Read the story.

1

Sheep walks on the beach. He passes a small bush near the shore.

2

He stops to look at a ship on the sea. He finds a shell.

3

He goes to the water and sees a fish. "It must enjoy the sea more than the fishbowl," he thinks.

4

He goes deeper and sees a shrimp. No, it's a jellyfish!

Say these words.
sheltered
cushion
bush
Can you hear the /sh/ sound?
Yes, I can!
Not sure.
No, I can't.

Theme: Sports

Sub-theme: Let's exercise

Term 2

/st/ sound: initial position
Extended learning: medial and final positions

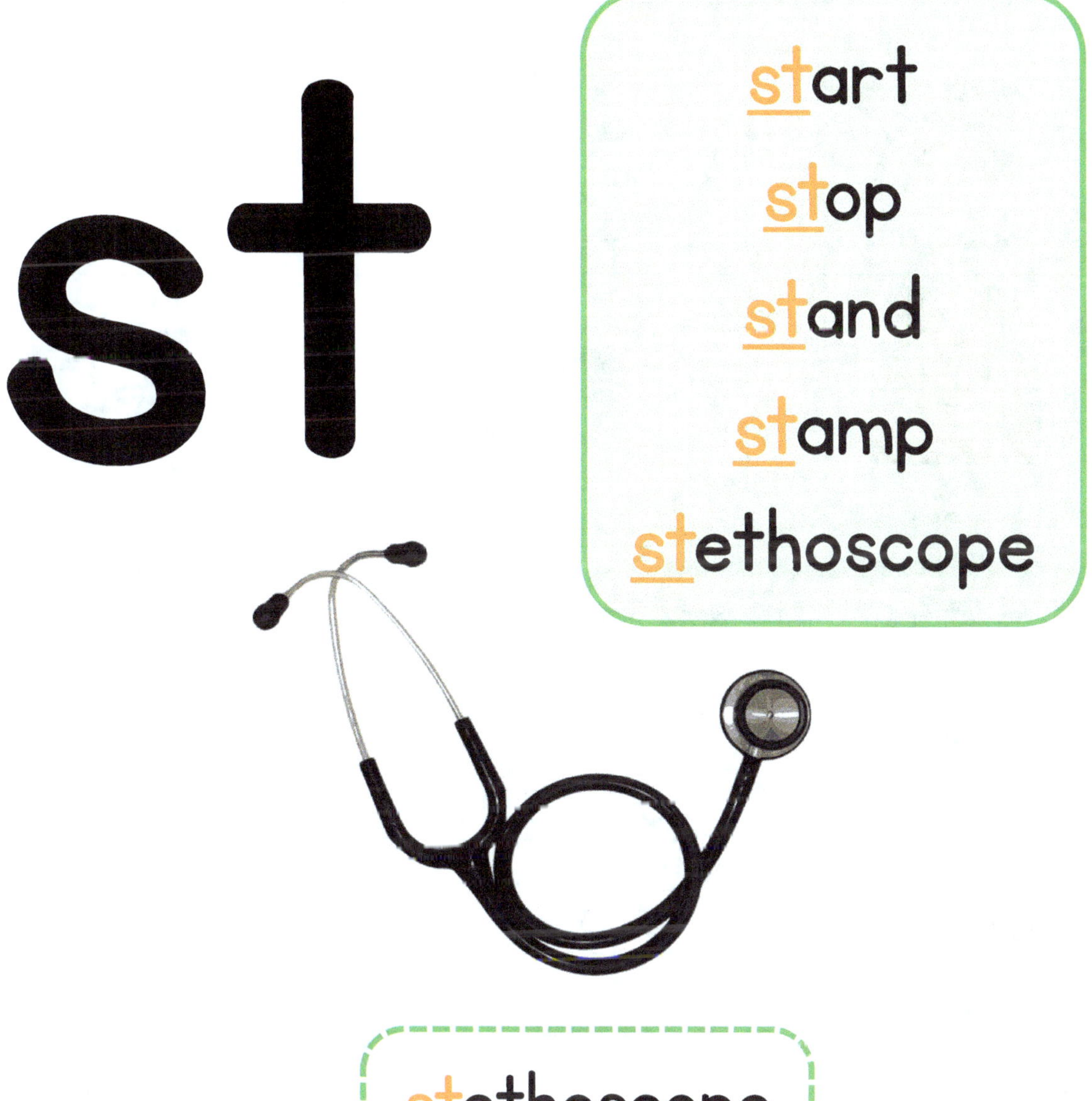

st

start
stop
stand
stamp
stethoscope

stethoscope

/st/ sound

1. Say my name. Point to each picture. Say its name.

2. Add my letters. Write the word. Circle the picture.

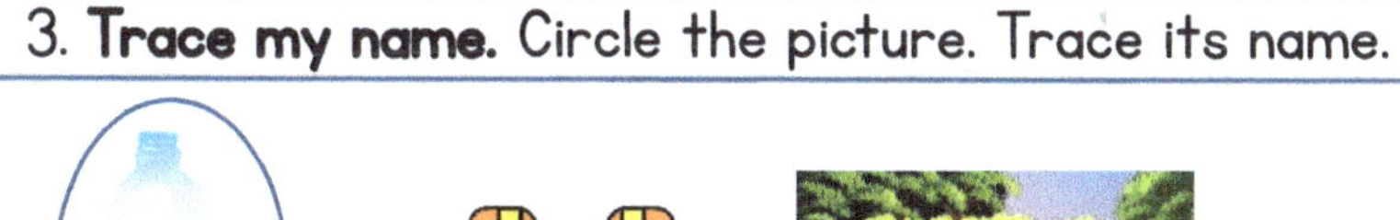

/st/ sound

3. **Trace my name.** Circle the picture. Trace its name.

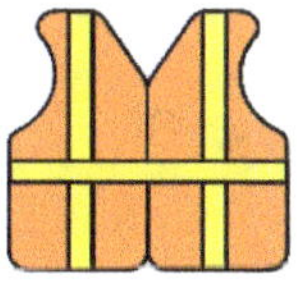

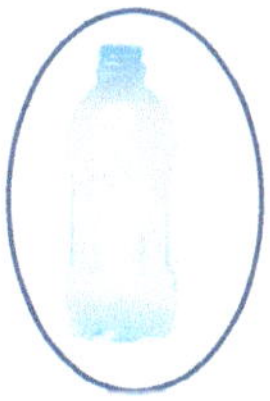

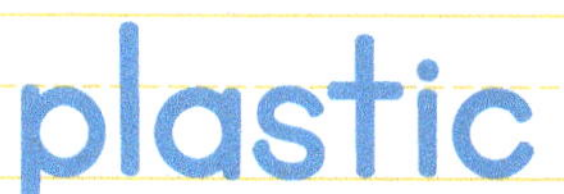

plastic

star

lobster

4. **Write my name.** Write the name in the sentence.

Put on the **vest.** 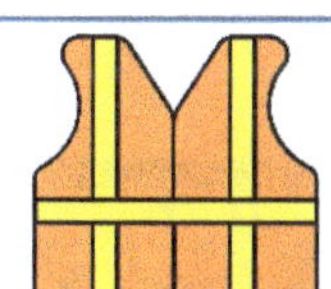

The ______ is hot. 

Birds are in the ______. 

/st/ sound

3. **Check me**. Look at the picture. Check the name. Write the name.

☐ s<u>t</u>ove   ☑ lob<u>st</u>er   ☐ ve<u>st</u>

lobster

☐ s<u>t</u>ool   ☐ fore<u>st</u>   ☐ pla<u>st</u>ic

☐ roo<u>st</u>er   ☐ <u>st</u>ar   ☐ ne<u>st</u>

4. **Read me**. Read the sentence.

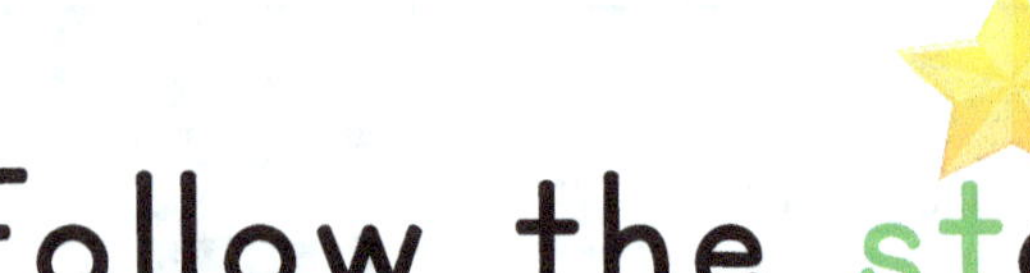

Follow the <u>st</u>ar to the ne<u>st</u>

in the fore<u>st</u>.

/st/ sound

Story words: artist, forest, lobsters, nest, star, stool, vest

7. **Read my story**. Look at the pictures. Read the story.

The artist sits on her stool. She is wearing a vest with lobsters on it.

She paints a castle in a forest. She paints a nest in a tree.

She paints the sky filled with stars.

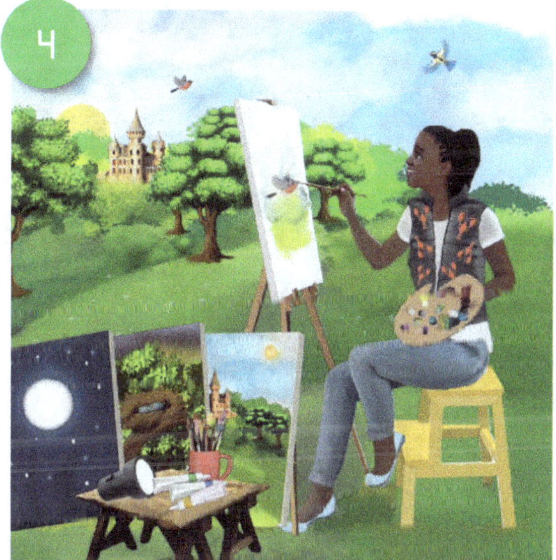

She paints and paints until the sun comes up.

Say these words.
plastic
stop
vest
Can you hear the /st/ sound?
Yes, I can!
Not sure.
No, I can't.

Term 3 — /th/ sound: initial position. Extended learning: final position

th

thank

think

Thursday

thumb

thumb

/th/ sound

1. Say my name. Point to each picture. Say its name.

thorn	**th**umb	**th**orn
thimble	ba**th**	**th**ief
slo**th**	too**th**	mou**th**

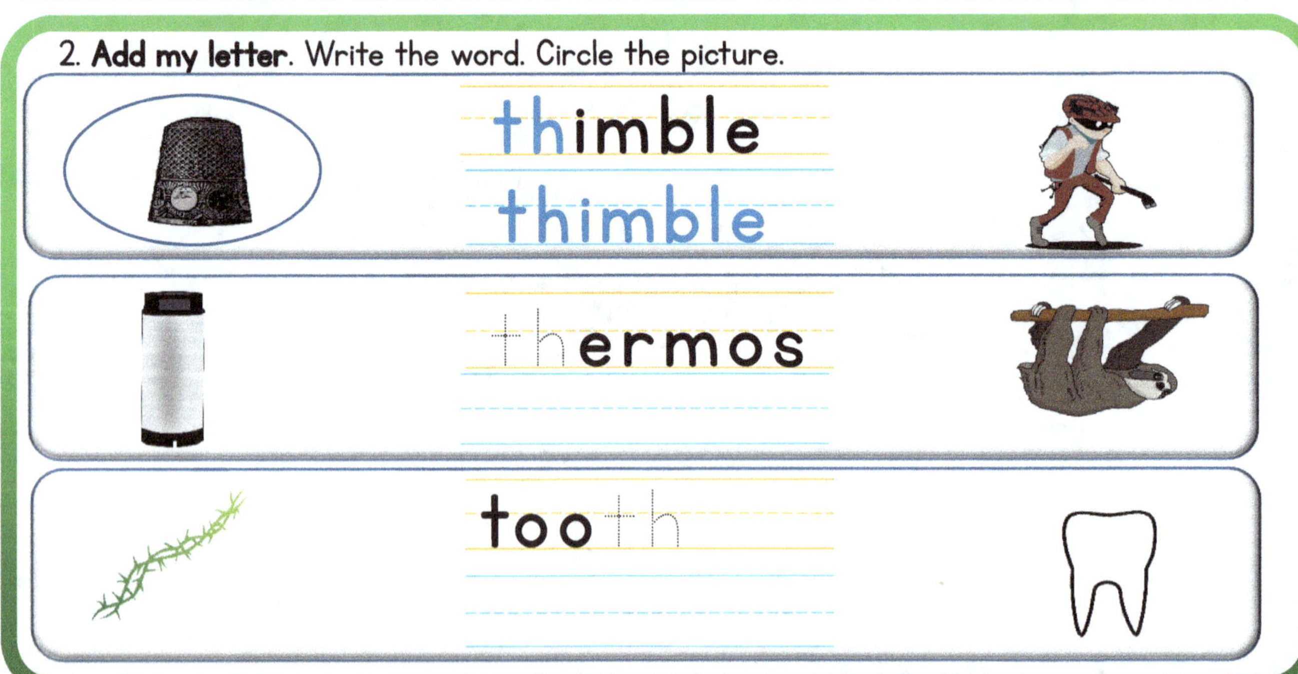

/th/ sound

3. Trace my name. Circle the picture. Trace its name.

 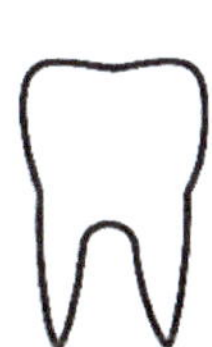 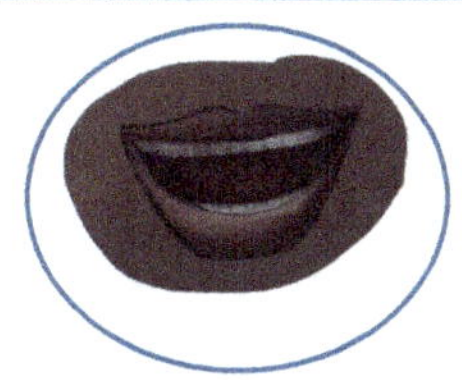

mouth

thumb

thorn

4. Write my name. Write the name in the sentence.

The thermos is hot. 

The __________ is slow. 

The __________ is in jail. 

/th/ sound

5. Check me. Look at the picture. Check the name. Write the name.

☐ **th**umb   ☑ mou**th**   ☐ **th**ief

mouth

☐ **th**imble   ☐ slo**th**   ☐ ba**th**

☐ **th**ermos   ☐ too**th**   ☐ **th**orn

6. Read me. Read the sentence.

Mother has a **th**imble on her

thumb.

/th/ sound

Story words: mouth, sloth, thorn, tooth

7. **Read my story.** Look at the pictures. Read the story.

Sloth opens his mouth and yawns. Oh my, he has lost a tooth.

"I need to show my parents," he says.

As he climbs the tree to go home, he pricks his thumb on a thorn.

"Ouch!" he says. But he is a brave little sloth and keeps going.

Say these words.
thank
thumb
tooth
Can you hear the /th/ sound?
Yes, I can!
Not sure.
No, I can't.

Yeah!
Hh
Super!
Amazing!
CHEETAH
Chasing and Capturing
Your Dreams with You
CONGRATULATIONS
YOU DID IT!
Presented to:
For:
completing the CHEETAH®
EARLY CHILDHOOD PHONICS 5+
Date:
Teacher/Caregiver:
WOW!
Cc
Dd
Ee
Ff
Great
Job!
Cool!
Gg
Bb
Aa
Jj
Awesome!
Wonderful!
Great!